The Dancer's
FOOT
BOOK

D0709042

The Dancer's
FOOT
BOOK

A Complete Guide to Footcare & Health for People who Dance

DR. TERRY L. SPILKEN

A Dance Horizons Book
Princeton Book Company, Publishers
Princeton, NJ

For my loving family:
Barbara, Rachel, Sarah, and Jaime
And in memory of my mother, Rachel

Copyright © 1990 by Princeton Book Company, Publishers

All rights reserved. No portion of this book may be reproduced
in any form or by any means without written permission of the
publisher.

A Dance Horizons Book
Princeton Book Company, Publishers
POB 57
Pennington, NJ 08534

Book Design by Anne O'Donnell
Cover Design by Olive Bryant
Typesetting by Peirce Graphic Services, Inc.
Editorial Supervisor: Roxanne Barrett

Library of Congress Cataloging-in-Publication Data

Spilken, Terry L.
      The dancers' foot book : a complete guide to footcare / by Terry
Spilken.
          p.   cm.
      "A Dance Horizons book"—T.p. verso
      Includes bibliographical references.
      ISBN 0-916622-97-5 : $24.95.—ISBN 0-916622-96-7 (pbk.)
      : $14.95
      1. Extremities, Lower—Wounds and injuries.   2. Extremi-
      ties,   Lower—Care and hygiene.   3. Dancers—Health and
      hygiene.
      I. Title.
      RD560.S65   1990
      617.5'85—dc20   89-64299
                                                                      CIP

CONTENTS

Audrey Connelly and Carld Jonaissant performing Songs of Mahler *by Michael Smuin for* The Dance Theatre of Harlem. *Photo by Marbeth.*

ACKNOWLEDGEMENTS

Many people deserve my thanks for helping to put this book together. Linda Baskt, Claudia Cohan Desmond, Penny Frank, Jodi Pam Krizer, Jean Scott, Fred Shilling, and Lucretia Welters directly contributed by writing certain sections. Their expertise and knowledge have greatly added to the merits of this book.

Eric Shonz's photographs and Roberta Robins Newman's illustrations are invaluable to understanding the text. Marbeth and Patrick Watson's professional photographs add beauty to the book.

Lisa Disort, Charles Farruggio, Patrick Leader, Stan Long, Melissa Roach, Lori Strelec, and Henrika Taylor modeled beautifully and should have very successful dancing careers ahead of them.

The Alvin Ailey American Dance Center, Jazzercise, Taffy's Dance Wear, and the International Dance and Exercise Association all provided assistance; Denise Jefferson and Arthur Miller deserve special thanks. Also Deana Danko, Danielle Mulvey, Laura Rowland and Lori Shilling deserve recognition for putting the book together.

Finally, I would like to thank all the dancers I have treated over the years. I find it extremely satisfying to help dancers. Seeing dancers through their injuries enables them to continue doing what they love best and allows them to create beauty for the rest of us.

Elisa Monte rehearsing Dreamtime *with the students of the Alvin Ailey American Dance Center. Photo by Marbeth.*

INTRODUCTION

"I could have danced all night!"
Allan Jay Lerner
"My Fair Lady"

One might imagine completing the above thought by saying ". . .if it weren't for the fact that my feet were killing me!" Of course, this was not what Eliza Doolittle had in mind, but many of us have had the experience of wanting to continue to dance, but simply finding it too uncomfortable or painful to do so because of our feet.

This book will offer information that will help you understand this critical part of your body. It is not only intended for the professional dancer, whose very career may depend on dancing all night, but for anyone who considers dance an important part of their lives. Understanding proper foot care, movement, and shoegear, and knowing as much as possible about your feet may help avoid injury or, at least, minimize injury.

Dancers use their bodies to express their art. To allow the body to speak, a dancer must understand it as best he or she can, thereby making maximum use of all it has to offer. Proper care begins at the bottom: the feet. The chapters that follow will review and explain important issues for the dancer. Read this book carefully. Knowledge of your feet and proper care could allow you many years of dancing without injury.

1

The human foot is a complicated package containing bones, muscles, tendons, ligaments, arteries, veins, and nerves. Whether a dancer is walking, running, or jumping, each part of the foot and leg must work together. To better maximize their performance, dancers should understand how their bodies function and the best ways to minimize injury. This book will attempt to explain how the foot and leg function, and what the dancer should know to achieve maximum performance.

It is estimated that over a lifetime, 87 percent of all Americans (or 189 million people) will at some time develop a foot problem. Out of every 1,000 disabilities, 20 stem from foot disorders. Combined, foot ailments are the third most crippling health problem after heart disease and cancer. Females suffer four times the number of foot problems as do males. It's no wonder that more than $200 million a year is spent on over-the-counter foot medications and appliances.

Doctors of Podiatric Medicine (DPM) are physicians whose specialty is the human foot. It is their responsibility to not only treat the vast numbers of foot problems that occur each year, but to try to prevent

Dance Theatre of Harlem. Children's tap dancing class performing at an open house. Photo by Marbeth.

problems from forming. Last year alone, the estimated 10,500 podiatrists practicing in the United States saw 35 million patients to treat more than 300 ailments of the human foot. The largest group of cases treated by podiatrists today are sports-related, a group that includes dancers.

As dancer-related activities increasingly appeal to a larger percentage of the population, podiatrists have noticed an increase in the types of injuries and their frequency. Children are starting dance classes at a very young age. People of all ages are dancing for fun. Dancers such as these generally are not trained in preventative measures that would minimize injury. The lack of understanding of how forces affect the foot has led to an increase in the number of injuries. The most common injuries affecting the foot and leg are: blisters; sprained ankles; tendonitis; periostitis (bone bruises); various fractures of bones in the foot; shin-splints (aching pain in the lower leg); heel spurs; and *plantar fasciitis* (separation of the thick fibrous layer on the bottom of the foot from the bones it cushions).

To understand the foot, one must first look at how it is constructed. The basic unit of support are the bones. Each foot contains 28 bones; both feet have about one-fourth of all the bones in the body. Nineteen different muscles or their tendons attach to these bones. A *tendon* is the band of tissue that connects the muscle to these bones. The action of these muscles and tendons causes the bones to move. Each step requires precise interaction of the muscle groups. There are 30 different joints in each foot and 112 to 117 ligaments holding the bones together in each foot. The ligaments cover each joint, adding stability for the bones. There are many yards of blood vessels and an intricate system of nerves. There is even 125,000 sweat glands in each foot. Everything is covered by tough connective and protective fascia. *Fascia* is a sheet or band of fibrous tissue.

The structure of the foot is designed to prevent unwanted motion that could lead to damage of an internal structure accompanied by pain. Pain is, of course, the body's signal that something is wrong, and should never be ignored. It is a warning to stop your dance activity and find out what is causing the problem. Continuing activity could lead to a more serious problem and a longer layoff from dancing.

Each time the foot hits the ground, it receives the force of two to three times your body weight. In one day, the foot endures hundreds of tons of impact in the roughly 8,000 to 10,000 steps you take. In a mile walk, you bear the gravity-induced impact of 700 to 800 pounds on each

Michael Jahoda during an Alvin Ailey American Dance Center Gala performance doing In Excelsis *by Penny Frank. The foot receives four times body weight landing from a jump. Photo by Marbeth.*

foot. When you run, the impact increases. A soccer player takes about 10,000 vigorous steps in a game; the impact on the player's foot exceeds 1,000 tons. During ballet, the dancer's foot receives a force four times the body's weight. While the foot is designed to take a person an average of 115,000 miles or four times around the earth in a lifetime, the repetitive insult to the foot by the dancer or athlete can cause injury. Combine the repetition with ill-fitting shoes, inadequate hygiene, biomechanical defects, hard surfaces, and inadequate preparation, and it's easy to understand the increase in foot injuries.

Improper treatment of an injury can lead to a chronic problem. Most dancers continue dancing, believing that their bodies will quickly lose physical strength if they stop. Instead of listening to the body, a dancer often ignores the warning signals and pays for it later. One problem untreated can lead to many problems endangering the dancer's future career. Eventually a dancer can be forced to stop dancing completely.

When one starts dance training, little is mentioned about what signs to look for to prevent injury from occurring. A dancer's discipline shouldn't just include attending classes regularly, following the proper diet, and wearing the proper attire. Dancers must discipline themselves to listen to their bodies. Such attention could reward them with a lifetime of dancing without pain.

Children at Alvin Ailey American Dance Center during a creative dance class. Photo by Marbeth.

One

FOOT GROWTH AND DEVELOPMENT IN YOUNG DANCERS

The foot develops and changes constantly during the first few years of life. The formation of bones, called *ossification*, takes about ten years for a girl and twelve years for a boy, but certain bones are not completely formed until the age of twenty. The last bones formed are the *sesamoids* and the base of the fifth *metatarsal*. The *calcaneus* doesn't fully develop until the age of six in a girl and age nine in a boy. Dance puts extra stress on young, growing bodies and ossification centers.

Dance training can also affect the development of the leg and the position of the knee. At birth, the legs appear bowed with a space between the knees *(genu varum)*. By a year-and-a-half to three years of age, the legs straighten, but between the ages of three and six, the knees appear closer together and the legs are in a knock-kneed position *(genu valgum)*. They straighten out again by age seven and remain straight until puberty. However, from puberty until the age of eighteen, the knees go back to the knock-kneed position before straightening as an adult.

A typical dance class for children should follow some set guidelines. First and foremost, it is imperative that no child be permitted to take class while wearing socks. Specific shoes for the dance form being studied should be worn, or no shoes if appropriate. If a child does not have the proper footwear, it is better for him or her to take class barefoot. The risk of injury while dancing in socks on a slippery floor is almost inevitable, but can be easily avoided.

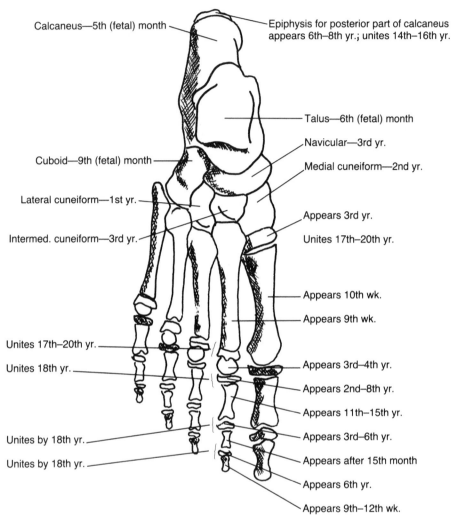

Calcaneus—5th (fetal) month

Epiphysis for posterior part of calcaneus appears 6th–8th yr.; unites 14th–16th yr.

Talus—6th (fetal) month

Navicular—3rd yr.

Cuboid—9th (fetal) month

Medial cuneiform—2nd yr.

Lateral cuneiform—1st yr.

Appears 3rd yr.

Intermed. cuneiform—3rd yr.

Unites 17th–20th yr.

Appears 10th wk.

Appears 9th wk.

Unites 17th–20th yr.

Unites 18th yr.

Appears 3rd–4th yr.

Appears 2nd–8th yr.

Appears 11th–15th yr.

Unites by 18th yr.

Appears 3rd–6th yr.

Unites by 18th yr.

Appears after 15th month

Appears 6th yr.

Appears 9th–12th wk.

Ossification chart of the bones of the foot

Dance shoes should always fit properly (see Chapter 2). There should always be room for the natural growth of the foot or its natural function. However, under no circumstances should there be extra room in the shoes, or the foot will not be able to function properly.

The class should always begin with warm-up exercises to minimize the possibility of injuries. This includes stretching and flexibility training. The next phase is the actual instruction, which for young children means

*Arthur Mitchell examining a child's foot development at a
Dance Theatre of Harlem audition. Photo by Marbeth.*

learning how their bodies move and how to balance from a center point.
For children aged seven or older, this technique training should
emphasize correct posture and body position. After working at the barre,
children are ready to work on center floor exercises. These include
walking, running, skipping, and jumping. As children develop an
awareness of movement, time could be allowed for improvisation. The
class should always end with cooling down exercises.

It is important to remember that for children learning to dance
there is a great demand on the lower body. In order to minimize injury
and undue strain, emphasis should be placed on proper alignment,
coordination of movements, correct anatomical position with straight
knees, strong ankles and feet, and finally, proper weight distribution.

Some points taught to children could avoid serious foot problems
later in life. Students must work to hold their feet evenly on the floor and
keep the toes stretched. "While the feet are bearing the weight of the
body they should be holding the ground at three points: one behind (the
back of the *calcaneus*); and two in front (the heads of the first and fifth
metatarsals). This triangle forms a base from which the muscles and soles
of the feet can work strongly in holding up the arch."[1] The strength to
control the placement of the feet is not confined to the lower extremities.
Essentially, placement begins with the head, followed by the back and

pelvis, and finishes with the thigh and leg. "A good teacher recognizes instinctively this interdependence of one part of the body to the other."[2]

In addition to the placement of the feet, several elementary movements require special attention. These include:

1. The feet should never sickle, especially in *demi-pointe* or *relevé*.

2. Children should not curl their toes to give the illusion of higher arches when pointing their feet.

3. A *demi-plié* should be taught to originate from the hips and children should not force it by pronating the feet.

4. A half-toe position should not be held for an extended period of time as it can be a major source of irritation to the bones in the feet.

5. The heel must remain on the floor as long as possible in *tendu* in order to properly stretch the leg and foot. When the heel and arch leave the floor, all the muscles in the ankle must stretch and the muscles under the instep should tighten slightly to avoid sickling the foot.

Because repetition of a harmful pattern could eventually distort the normal foot alignment and lead to injuries it is important to keep these guidelines in mind when teaching children.

Children also need to be taught the extremely important part the knees play in protecting the body from injury. They are pedestals of support for the body's weight and serve as an intermediary for the weight on the feet. Knees should always be straight and aligned with hips and feet, but never be in a locked position.

In ballet, a 180-degree rotation or turnout is the main objective, but this should be accomplished from the hips, not from the knees and feet, as is sometimes practiced. If children cannot rotate their hips enough, they will compensate by forcing their knees and ankles out. Moreover, to accomplish fifth position, which is the most difficult to execute, children tend to bend their knees. A bent knee, besides being weak and aesthetically unappealing, will continue to exert extra pressure on the joints, causing knee instability and strain on the ligaments.

Many times, however, bent knees are necessary. A *demi-plié* requires the knees to bend and therefore must done in moderation. A teacher should avoid having children sit at the lowest point of a *plié* so

I first saw Eleanor at the age of eighteen. She had severe pain in the first *metatarsal phalangeal* joint, primarily in her right foot. When she woke up in the morning it was stiff and painful, at the height of discomfort for the day. As Eleanor walked, the aching eased within 10 to 15 minutes. However, the pain returned as she danced, especially when in *relevé.* Her condition was diagnosed as osteoarthritis.

Eleanor's first *metatarsal* joint showed a great amount of deterioration with a narrowing of the joint space. A complete dance history revealed that she started dancing school at the age of four and began studying *pointe* when she was eight years old. Eleanor believes that the teachers put the children on *pointe* at an early age to make an impression on the children's parents.

Unfortunately, the growth plates in Eleanor's feet had not closed by the time she was eight. By dancing on *pointe* before the bones could withstand the force, she had caused great damage to her feet. As a result, she is stricken with a chronically painful condition. Eleanor is in her twenties now and I have kept her dancing with various conservative treatments. In spite of her chronic condition and resulting pain, she still chooses to dance.

that they will not drop their body weight, thus forcing the body out of alignment. A good *demi-plié* must be even and flowing on the descent as well as the ascent, as undue pressure could lead to ligament and cartilage damage.

Dancing on *pointe* also can be harmful to children. It is better, both physically and mentally, not to begin *pointe* work with children too soon. Children should be at least eleven or twelve years old before attempting to study *pointe.* At that age, the bones should be in their proper

Allow children their differences due to changes in development at various ages. Proper teaching is essential so damage is not done to the young dancer's body. Homer Bryant at Dance Theatre of Harlem School auditions. Photo by Marbeth.

positioning and formed to withstand the tremendous force exerted upon them.

Before beginning *pointe* classes, children also should have completed a sufficient amount of training; usually four to five years is recommended. By that time children should have learned proper alignment and technique so the feet have had a chance to develop and strengthen. It is important, too, for the arches to be strong enough to support the body weight.

Another aspect to consider when thinking about teaching a child *pointe* is that wearing a toe shoe will be more comfortable if the first three toes are approximately the same length. If this is so, balancing will be easier because of the stability and support provided by the three even toes.

Depending on their anatomy and physique, children will adapt to training differently. As they continue to develop under a competent teacher's guidance, the chance of injuries should be minimal. Most of the problems which are experienced, such as muscle cramps and fatigue, are very common yet not serious. Proper rest for a day or two with typical home remedies are effective in healing these maladies. It is important to see a doctor, however, if a more serious problem occurs.

April Berry performing Cry by Alvin Ailey. Photo by Marbeth.

Two

SPECIAL
CONSIDERATIONS
FOR DANCERS

The type of training a dancer receives often can lead to problems. Different types of dance use different muscles and body positions. Ballet dancers develop their bodies to absorb specific forces and punishment that are quite different than the forces exerted on a modern dancer who is dancing barefoot. In the same manner, ballet and modern dancers receive different training than jazz or tap dancers wearing a hard-soled shoe.

Because of these differences, many problems can arise in going from class to class. Varying the type of dance you do can put undo stress on different areas of the body. Staying in the best physical condition is the best way to prepare for these various assaults. Proper body strength will lessen the chance of strain on the body. Proper stretching and flexibility training also is vital. It will especially help dancers who vary the type of dancing they do each day as part of their training.

Choosing the correct shoegear is also vitally important to the health of dancers' feet. In order for a shoe to fulfill its function, it must fit properly. Many shoe dealers are concerned more with sales than with proper fitting. Many are not trained in measurement techniques, so it is up to dancers themselves to decide how a shoe fits. In general, given the choice between a slightly larger or slightly smaller shoe, select the larger shoe; if one foot is larger than the other, choose the larger size.

When being measured for shoes, compare the sitting and standing size of the foot. Most measuring devices measure three things: length from

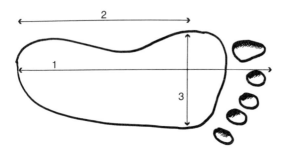

Three ways to measure for proper shoe fit: 1. Heel to toe length   2. Heel to ball of the foot at the widest point of the forefoot   3. Width at widest point of the forefoot

heel to longest toe, heel to the ball of the foot, and width. It is best to fit the foot from the heel to the ball of the foot, rather than the toe, especially if you have a "Morton's" foot (short first *metatarsal*). The heel counter (cup around the heel) should fit snugly yet not be so stiff as to cause irritation. A loose fitting counter can cause blisters or possible tendon irritation from excessive motion. The vamp of the shoe (the part that covers the forefoot) should be wide enough to accommodate the forefoot without being too loose (causing blisters) or too tight (causing corns, toe deformities, and cramping of the muscles). The toe box should allow free movement of the toes without pressure. Pointed toes or toe boxes that slope can cause irritation to nails and digits themselves. Also, toes should not strike the end of the shoe. Remember that feet can swell during long dance routines and rehearsals. Any shoe that does not fit correctly can cause severe problems in the future.

BALLET

Ballet slippers should fit snugly. Make sure there is no room in front of the toes. There should be elastic at the instep to hold them in place.

When buying toe shoes, make sure they are a good brand. They should be made for quality. Proper fit is essential; custom work can be done to individualize the shoe. Pick a heavier toe box when you first start *pointe* work. It should be stiff and strong. Use lambswool in the front of the shoe to cushion the toes.

Custom work can personalize a dance shoe so many problems can be avoided. Shoes can have arches added, elastic adjusted, or be reshanked or reblocked.

Because of the many different types offered, ballet shoes are the hardest shoes to fit. The first thing that must be explained is the difference between soft ballet slippers and *pointe* or toe slippers. A soft ballet shoe is made of either leather or canvas, or a "stretch" satin. The toe is pleated into the sole of the shoe and has a soft leather platform or shank. They are usually lined in leather and often have a suede insole or "sock." They are completely flexible and can be rolled into a ball. They have a drawstring made of either cloth or elastic and stay on the foot by attaching elastic across the instep of the foot.

A *pointe* or toe shoe has a hard box front and a hard shank usually made of durable paper. The material most often used in making a toe shoe is satin, but the shoes can be made of leather or canvas as well. The toe is pleated and the shoe has a drawstring of either cloth or elastic. The box of the shoe is made of "Hessian" or burlap cloth with a water soluble glue, which is what gives the shoe its wooden appearance.

To fit both ballet flats and *pointe* shoes, certain rules should be followed. Both ballet slippers and *pointe* shoes should fit snugly. This is one reason why parents find ballet so expensive. One cannot fit dance shoes to allow for growth! The softer quality leather slippers generally stretch a great deal, thereby lasting through a growth period. A ballet slipper, though snug, should not be too tight at the heel nor should the toes cross. You should be able to place all of your toes flat when standing, and the ball of your foot should be flat on the floor when on *demi-pointe*.

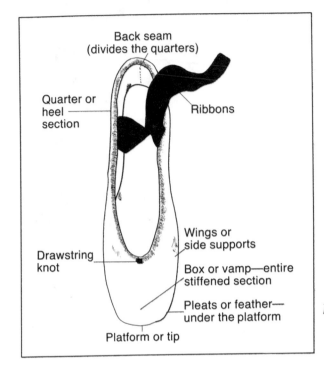

Back seam
(divides the quarters)

Quarter or
heel
section

Ribbons

Drawstring
knot

Wings or
side supports

Box or vamp—entire
stiffened section

Pleats or feather—
under the platform

Parts of the pointe shoe

Platform or tip

When you buy ballet flats, you should be given some elastic to be sewn into the shoe. The elastic should be sewn at the spot where the heel, when compressed, forms a right angle with the side of the shoe and then only below the drawstring. The purpose of the elastic is to hold the heel of the shoe to the foot.

Pointe shoes are especially difficult to fit. A fitting mistake is usually a costly one. It is not unusual for a dancer to buy two pairs at the same time to accommodate differently sized feet. A dancer also finds that shoes will last longer if two pairs are alternated, allowing each pair time to dry out between wearings.

A proper fit is one in which the shoe is quite snug, allowing the toes to move slightly but not "wiggle." The ball of the foot is flat on the ground while in a resting position and in *demi-pointe*. The top of the shoe lies flat across the top of the foot. In other words, you should not be able to insert your fingers into the top of the shoe. There should not be a gap when on *pointe*; you should not be able to pinch the material at the back of the heel. When flat, the heel of the shoe should not dig into the heel of the foot. The shoe should be tight all over but tolerable, both flat and on *pointe*.

When Susie came to me for treatment she was sixteen years old and had been taking dance classes since age eight. She started *pointe* work at age fourteen. Her problem was pain in the big toe of her right foot. She would begin experiencing discomfort after taking *pointe* class. The pain was in the area under the *hallux* (big toe) nail. The nail would become black and on occasion the entire nail would fall off.

Examination revealed no pathology or anatomical variations to the *hallux*. Her gait analysis and biomechanical exam were also within normal limits. The problem had to be in her *pointe* work or shoe. Her shoes fit correctly and she was using lambswool. When she went up on *pointe*, however, I was able to see the problem.

Susie was bending the big toe of her right foot at the first proximal *interphalangeal* joint. By plantarflexing the *hallux*, she was putting a tremendous force and the weight of her body onto the nail. The force was causing her black nail and pain. This is commonly referred to as "dancer's toe."

Susie had to adjust the position of her *hallux* when on *pointe*. We created a splinting effect using lambswool placed on the plantar of the big toe, which made it difficult for her to plantarflex her toe. She also had to retrain herself to eliminate this painful habit she had gotten into while on her right foot. She has since stopped this practice and has not had a recurrence of the black nail.

A shoe with a low heel is preferable to one with a high heel. It gives a smooth line and also keeps from digging into the very sensitive Achilles tendon. When a shoe is cut low in the heel it often slips off. This makes it necessary to use elastic attached at the back (on the outside) as well as using a small elastic loop at the back of the heel through which ribbons are run.

A *pointe* shoe cannot be fit for durability. The choice of an extra hard shank for a beginning dancer often can prevent the foot from developing the muscles it needs for strength and stamina on *pointe.*

Points on Fitting

IS IT TOO BIG?

1. If there is a space between the drawstring knot and the foot.

2. If the shoe twists off at the heel.

3. If it is baggy at the heel.

4. If the foot slips forward.

5. If the foot is rolling around in the shoe.

IS IT TOO SMALL?

1. If the toes are pressed, bent or sore inside the shoe.

2. If the toes are pressed against the tip inside the shoe.

IS IT JUST RIGHT?

1. If the toe is just touching the inside of the platform.

2. If the sides of the foot are being supported without pain. Slight pressure is alright.

3. If the heel stays in the shoe on *demi-pointe.*

4. If there is settling rather than slipping in.

To fit the *pointe* shoe correctly, you must first stand in second position. Relax the foot muscles and spread your toes and then gently *demi-plie.* The *demi-plie* position *à la seconde* stretches the foot, toes, and heels to their longest point. This allows you to ask the following questions: Are your toes touching the inside of the block? Is there any pressure on the sides or the top of the foot from the shoe? Is there any pressure across the *metatarsal* joints or bunion area? Your toes should be just very slightly touching the inside of the block. There should be no undue pressure or pain on the sides of the toes, the top of the toes, or across your *metatarsal* or bunion joints. If you spread out the shoe a little bit by pressing down on the box, this will allow a little bit more space across your bunion joint, but there should be no pain. The general fitting is tight but not sore.

Photo courtesy of Gamba Shoe Co.

Place your foot on *pointe*, not arched. The reason you do this is because when you go into a store to get fitted for *pointe* shoes, you may be cold and if you have not warmed up and go straight on *pointe*, you could do some damage to the fine muscles and possibly your joints. Is your big toe or your second toe touching the inside of the platform that you are standing on? Is it touching or is it pressing? The answer is that it should just be touching. If it is pressing, then your shoe is either too big and you are sliding forward, or the shoe could be too short and you are being pressed into the shoe.

It is important to look at the shoe itself now if you are just settling into it. The sides of the shoe are in fact what support you when you are on *pointe*, so these should be tight but not cause soreness. You should be able to touch the inside of the shoe with your toe. There should be no undue pressure other than this normal pressure of being held inside the shoe, and there should be no baggy heels. The result is that when you go on *pointe*, you will be supported completely by the shoe and in turn your foot will support the shoe.

Your foot supports the shoe and the shoe supports your foot. You do not need elastic on the heel because the heel should be fitting firmly. If your ribbons are placed correctly, they should hold the heel onto the foot. It is not suggested that you use any kind of padding inside the shoe as this upsets the balance of the shoe. If the shoe is fitting correctly, it will protect your foot. You do not need padding as this will mean you would need to get a bigger shoe to fit in the padding and therefore you will not get a correct fit and you will find it difficult to balance on a shoe that is too big for you or too wide for you, so make sure that you get the right width and the right length and you will have a long, safe, happy, and comfortable career as a dancer.

MODERN

Modern dance poses many unique problems. Unlike most other dancers, the modern dancer does not wear a covering over the foot. Without a shoe, the foot is exposed to a great amount of friction against the floor. More than

Students of the Alvin Ailey American Dance Center performing Gazelle *by George Faison. Photo by Marbeth.*

Peter is a twenty-four-year-old modern dancer who dances with a well-known company. He sprained his ankle during a rehearsal and then tried to treat his injury himself. After two weeks he came to my office.

Peter's ankle injury was not very serious—it was a secondary sprain—but he had not treated it properly. He would not put any strapping or other bandages on his foot because he did not want anything showing while he performed. The only way to allow the ligaments to heal in such a case is with external stability and rest, so physical therapy and medication alone would not improve his ankle. He needed a strong strapping of his ankle to limit movement and allow the ligament to rest.

In this case, I not only had to treat Peter's injury, but I also had to use a psychological approach to convince him to follow my treatment plan. I stressed to Peter that without proper treatment, his minor injury could become major. Scar tissue could form where the ligament was damaged, which could lead to a small loss in his range of motion of his ankle joint. That loss could affect his ability to dance.

The solution was to wear a strapping over the ankle for up to two weeks. Peter began physical therapy and rested the ankle as much as possible. The strapping allowed him to continue dancing without aggravating his injury. Peter used skin-colored makeup to cover the tape. In ten days, he was able to use an ankle brace during the day and perform without any covering. In three weeks he was completely healed.

other dancers, the modern dancer is prone to blisters, calluses, and abrasions.

Treating the modern dancer also poses a unique challenge. Often a bandage, padding, or strapping is applied to the dancer's foot. Without a shoe, the material is visible while the dancer is performing. I have treated many modern dancers who would not allow me to apply tape to feet for this reason. Obviously, this delays healing of an injury. The only solution is to try to mask the bandage. The dancer can apply body makeup to cover the material. Skin-colored makeup will usually do a good job at making the material invisible to an audience.

Dance surfaces are also extremely important. Floor surfaces can cause damage to a dancer's feet. While all dancers are affected by the surface they dance on, the modern dancer is more susceptible to problems with flooring because they are barefoot.

Dancing on hard surfaces lacking any give is dangerous to the lower extremity. Even so, many dance classes are conducted on a concrete slab. It also is a problem to dance on a surface that is too soft. Thick carpet with a foam base offers no lateral stability. The ankle has a tendency to roll, making ankle sprains more likely.

In general, wooden floors offer the best lateral foot stability. The floor should be resilient and have a spring-like effect to absorb force. Concrete, asphalt, cement, and other pavements are very unforgiving on the feet. Dancers who perform on city streets or in parks on hard pavements are more susceptible to traumatic injuries.

A dance floor that absorbs force reduces the fatigue element so common for dancers. Less force has to be absorbed by the knee, the primary shock absorber of the body, when the force is going into the give of the floor. After all, the dancer landing from a jump creates a force equal to four times his or her body weight. If the floor does not absorb some of that force, it will go back into the lower extremity. That type of force not only affects the knee but also can injure the ankle, hip, back, or neck.

·The floor surface should be smooth without being slippery. Any uneven area can cause injury. The floor surface should not affect the dancer's balance. Always check the flooring before dancing. Leaving any water, powder, rosin, sand, or other material on the floor simply is inviting problems.

JAZZ AND TAP

Jazz shoes are made out of a variety of materials, from hard nappa leather to the finest quality doeskin. The bottom of the shoe can be either rubber or suede. The shoe can also be flexible with a collapsible heel or nonflexible with a stitched-down heel.

Jean was a dancer whose specialty was tap. He developed a lesion on the plantar surface of his left foot, under the second *metatarsal* head. While tapping, the pain became very sharp. Normal walking and most other forms of dance only caused mild discomfort. Jean thought he had formed a callus or a corn.

My examination revealed the lesion to be a wart. Warts are caused by the *papova* virus. The most common treatment is surgical correction, but Jean was not a good candidate for surgery. He did not want to miss seven to ten days of dancing. We decided to treat his wart conservatively, allowing him to continue dancing and tap without disruption.

Once a week Jean would come to the office. I would debride as much of the wart as possible, a procedure that involves hardly any pain. I would then apply a very strong medication. At home every day, Jean would apply a prescription wart medication. The pain while tapping diminished almost immediately. We continued this treatment for about eight weeks until the wart was completely gone. Jean did not miss one dance class.

For the novice, choosing a jazz shoe is often difficult. There are several ways to tell if the shoe is right or wrong. First, when toes are pointed, does the sole of the shoe cling to the arch of the foot? Second, when standing flat, is the heel of the foot squarely in the center of the heel of the shoe? Lastly, when on half-toe (or *relevé*) is the ball of the foot flat on the floor, or does the foot feel as though it has a dent in the center of the ball? A shoe that does not satisfy in these three areas will never be right. It probably will rip from the strain on the leather before the shoe ever stretches enough to be comfortable.

Jazz shoes come in several styles. The classic jazz shoe is a lace-up flat with a chrome (suede) sole, a rubber sole, or a stitched suede sole with

Shaun Edgar Jones performing at Alvin Ailey American Dance Center June Gala. Photo by Marbeth.

a rubber heel. Each has its advantages and disadvantages. For the most part, shoes with stitched soles and rubber heels are not very flexible and the stitching wears out quickly unless rosin is applied for protection.

Today, the most popular jazz flats are those with rubber soles. At first it might seem to you that the rubber sole will hamper your ability to turn, but after a short time the rubber wears down enough to make that motion easy. Rubber soles also take longer to wear out and require no rosin to prevent slipping.

Other types of shoes used for jazz range from a tiny strap of leather with a half sole to Grecian sandals (a T-strap flexible shoe with a soft suede bottom), to a lace-up soft leather boot. The type of jazz dancing that you are doing usually determines the type of shoe needed. Some female dancers find that taking class and rehearsing in a higher-heeled shoe makes stage dancing and auditioning easier. Females more often dance in shoes that have at least a two-inch heel.

Jazz shoes with heels fall into the character shoe category. Character shoes are shoes that fit into every category of dancing. They are used for ballet, jazz, tap, ballroom, folk, and ethnic dance. The basic character shoe for women is a heeled shoe with the heel ranging from one-and-a-half inches to three inches in height.

David was performing in a Broadway show. Because the show was set in the 1700s, David wore tight-fitting boots with a heel. The stage was pitched on an angle facing the audience.

David started experiencing very sharp pain in his right heel after being in the show several months. His heel hurt in the morning when he got out of bed. The pain eased after he walked for about ten minutes. As the day went on, however the pain got worse. Performing in the boot on the slanted stage made the pain intolerable.

A series of X-rays revealed a heel spur with bursitis in the right foot. A biomechanical exam and gait analysis showed that because of his anatomical structure, David was pronating excessively.

To control his abnormal foot structure and excessive movement, biomechanical orthotic devices were made. Because 95 percent of all patients with heel spurs respond to conservative treatment and do not need surgical correction, I believed the orthotics would control the chronic nature of his condition.

To treat the acute pain of the bursitis, I started David on physical therapy. He received three theraputic injections, each a week apart, coupled with anti-inflammatory medication. Under this treatment plan, his condition improved immediately. After about eight weeks, he was completely asymptomatic, and he has not had a reoccurrence of heel pain. He still uses the orthotics in his everyday shoes and during a performance on stage.

A shoe with a heel higher than one-and-a-half inches should have a braceable heel. Braces are small brackets that are placed between the heel and the sole of the shoe and hammered in to keep the heel from breaking off. A shoe should also have a layer of "cat's-paw" rubber applied to the sole and heel of the shoe. The rubber should be attached as far as the instep of the shoe so that it will not peel off easily. The rubber protects the soft leather sole and keeps the stitching from wearing out too quickly. At the same time, it keeps the bottom of the shoe from becoming too slick.

Tap shoes come in every imaginable shape from high-button boots to sneakers. The important thing to remember about tap shoes is the fit of the tap to the shoe. The more space the tap covers the better. The toe tap must be flush with the end of the shoe and fit "straight" across. That goes for heels as well.

AEROBIC DANCING

Dancing as a form of exercise has been gaining in popularity. In 1987, it was estimated that more than 22 million people were performing dance exercise at over 20,000 facilities.

Exercise put to music can take many differents formats. Aerobics, slimnastics, jazz exercise or Jazzercise, and dance workouts are all exercise programs put to music. The reason for its popularity is simple: it is fun, so the monotony of working out is reduced.

In aerobic dancing, the emphasis shifts from muscle size and strength to increased flexibility, endurance, coordination, and improved working of the cardiopulmonary system. Basically, in aerobic dancing you are increasing the body's ability to use oxygen. The heart will beat stronger, so with fewer beats, the heart can deliver the same amount of oxygen through the blood. Therefore, your heart has more time to rest between beats. While performing aerobics, the heart rate will increase. The body's need for oxygen increases, so the heart pumps faster to achieve this. Thus, the heart becomes more efficient at pumping blood. The exercise program will also improve a person's metabolism. Weight loss can occur from the exercise itself and the better metabolic rate. Your pulse and blood pressure should also be lowered and your lungs should work to full capacity.

Aerobics is a flexible exercise. It can be achieved by many other activities besides dancing. Some include brisk walking, running, jumping, kicking, and jogging. Dance exercise does not depend on the weather or team participants. It can be performed in a fitness center or at home. The important element for cardiovascular fitness is consistency. The activity should last about 30 minutes and be done at least every other day. All that is really needed is the music and a good pair of aerobic shoes.

Many dance programs consist of one hour of activity. There is a warmup, 30 minutes of aerobics and then a cool-down. Warmup and cool-down are necessary to dissipate the lactic acid that is forming in the

Carlos is a ballet dancer who injured his ankle two years ago and has had chronic pain ever since. His problem began when he tried to self-treat his condition.

Carlos tried to strengthen his injured ankle through exercise. He decided to perform aerobic dance exercises and used weights on his wrists and ankles. Unfortunately, not only did his ankle get worse, he started to experience knee pain.

Performing high-impact aerobics caused excessive pressure on Carlos's ankle. Because he never received proper treatment, scar tissue formed in the injured ligaments. The scar tissue caused his pain and a limitation of motion. Aerobic dancing caused more damage, and the use of weights compounded the problem. The weights added a great force that was exerted into Carlos's knees.

Once treatment started for Carlos, he stopped the aerobic dancing. Physical therapy and injection therapy helped in breaking up some of the fibrosis and scar tissue in the ligaments of his ankle. I put him on a flexibility program to stretch the muscles in his leg and foot. He also used heat as often as possible. Within a few weeks, he saw improvement. He had less pain in his ankle when he danced. He also increased the range of motion in his ankle joint. His knee improved as soon as he stopped the aerobics. Surgery is the only way to attempt to restore Carlos's ankle, but it has not been necessary. He can dance with only a slight limitation of movement and minimal discomfort.

muscles as a byproduct of the exercise. Lactic acid will cause the muscle to fatigue.

Aerobic dance activities are divided into low-impact and high-impact activities. In low-impact areobics, one foot is always on the floor. Skipping, for example, can be done with low impact. Jumping, on the other hand, is a high-impact activity; both feet are off the ground. Obviously, high-impact aerobics have a much greater injury rate, because

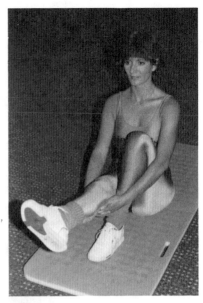

Jean Scott demonstrating
some basic warm-up and
cool-down stretches. It is
very important that these
movements be done before
and after aerobic dancing.

of the increased force on the joints and the need for greater shock absorption.

Dance programs can also be geared to different age groups. For younger participants, the program should include more dance and less aerobics. The dance program should be fun, and brief, to accommodate children's shorter attention spans.

Children are more flexible and have increased energy levels. Still, a warmup and cool-down are necessary. Activities could include isolation of muscles, across-the-floor movement, front and back movements, proper body alignment, and coordination with repetition. There should be little jumping and no trauma. All the activities should lead to a performance.

Seniors can do a modified version of dance exercise. It should be less strenuous with less repetition of each movement. This type of program can be modified for the handicapped, postoperative patients, and pregnant woman. Increased flexibility should be a benefit for all people in this category. Less force should be exerted on the joints, and activities should always be low impact. The choreographed routines should have no jumping, hopping, or skipping. The appeal of aerobics is that it is noncompetitive. Pace yourself and modify the program to your own individual needs.

After you first start a dance exercise program it will take a while for you to get into shape. It will take at least five to six weeks to really learn the program and start getting into shape. Try to participate every other day. This will allow your body one day's rest between workouts.

Correct body alignment and position are essential. Stand tall with your knees and feet facing forward. After a landing, make sure your heels touch the ground. Do not land with your legs and knees straight; bend the knee to help absorb the force. If you do not bend your knees enough you could put excessive force on your back. The knees should not extend too far out over the toes, or you will put increased pressure on the *patellae.*

Do not overextend while flexing or extending during the workout. You should be working first one muscle group and then another; this should avoid overuse syndromes. Overuse occurs from repetitive stress to a mechanically inefficient musclature, and cramps are a common result. They are caused by fatigue, poor diet, or a lack of fluids. Proper choreographed routines should vary the work done by the various muscle groups. Lunge with your body weight evenly distributed. Correct body alignment is essential. Use a pelvic tilt when performing a *plié.* If any injury occurs, give your body time to rebuild its strength. Follow your doctor's and teacher's advice.

The dancer will become healthier with an aerobics exercise program. The warmup and cool-down are essential. Stretching prevents injury (see Chapter 4). Stretching also can be used to heal from an injury. Individualize the stretching programs to meet your needs. Try to isolate each muscle group and use each area separately.

With time, you will develop increased stamina and strength. There will be an increase in calcium uptake of the bones and increased flexibility. You will feel better, look better, and be in a better health.

Wearing the proper shoegear is the most important factor in avoiding injury. The shoe should only be used for aerobics, and should be replaced approximately every six months. Look for good inside support with a removable insole. When necessary, a podiatrist will recommend sports orthotics for proper biomechanical control (see Chapter 6). The shoe should have extra protection in the front and across the toe box. Aerobic shoes generally are heavily cushioned and provide protection for stress points. High tops offer more support but are more restrictive of ankle movement. Do not get shoes made of soft glove leather; they won't give enough support. The shoe should be flexible at the *metatarsal phalangeal* joints, where the foot bends.

Wear proper socks when trying on shoes. Socks should be heavy enough to provide protection. While dancing, some people like to wear two pairs of socks for additional protection. A sock should be made of natural fibers (cotton or wool), which absorb perspiration better. Tights can be worn under the sock. Tights come in footless, stirrups, or full foot styles. Footless tights usually are best and allow the sock to protect the foot and absorb moisture. Support tights made of lycra or spandex are also available.

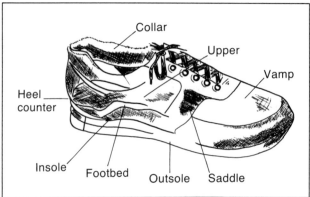

Parts of the aerobic shoe

The floor surface is also extremely important. Always try to dance on a surface with give. The softer the floor, the less impact into the ankle, knee, and leg. Hardwood floors have a lot of give; and carpeting also helps. A shock-resistant surface is also an advantage. Ideally, a gym floor with underlying springs provides shock absorption and stability. Concrete is the worst surface, even covered with carpeting. Tile is also a nonresilient surface.

If you must dance on concrete or tile, warm up thoroughly, stretch the muscles adequately, and keep a slight bend in the knee to absorb some of the force. To minimize the force of impact always use the full foot, not just the ball of the foot. Land on the toes, and shift your body weight to the ball of the foot and and then to the heel as the foot reaches the ground. Be sure the heel makes contact with the ground. To avoid stubbing the toes or tripping, make sure you fully lift the foot.

To keep a low injury rate, then, remember these pointers: always use the proper aerobic shoegear, try to dance only on the correct floor surface, and follow the instructions given by your teacher. There should be no pain during a workout. If something starts to hurt, stop. After the cool-down, a hot shower or bath will soothe the body.

Arabesque demonstrated by the Alvin Ailey American Dance Center children's ballet class. Photo by Marbeth.

Three

DANCE MOVEMENTS AND ASSOCIATED INJURIES

ARABESQUE. A pose that creates an elongated line by standing on one leg and extending the other behind, either on or off the floor. The supporting leg may be straight or in *demi-plié*, but the weight of the leg must remain evenly distributed over the whole foot. The working leg must be stretched with a straight knee. While performing any of the many variations of an arabesque, it is important to keep the weight of the body evenly distributed on the supporting foot to avoid any discomfort or injury. If too much force is put into the arch of the supporting leg, *plantar fasciitis* can occur. This same pronatory force can lead to heel bursitis or a more chronic heel spur may develop. In the *demi-plié* position, excessive force can be absorbed by the Achilles tendon and tendonitis may occur.

ASSEMBLÉ. An elevation step done by brushing one foot outward on the floor and then in the air while at the same time springing upward with the supporting foot. The body must be erect and centered over the hips and feet to do an *assemblé* so that when the foot brushes outward no undue stress is caused by trying to compensate for the uneven weight distribution. Also, proper body alignment is necessary so the supporting foot can get a good spring off the floor. If either foot needs to make adjustments, an injury may occur. The supporting foot can receive undo force through the ankle, resulting in a sprain. The acting foot can be irritated by the brushing motion, leading to abrasions of the skin, blistering, contusions, or *hematomas*. Improper landing can also cause *periostitis* to occur. It is also important for the legs to remain turned out throughout the movements of the *assemblé* so as not to cause strain on the knee during takeoff or landing.

ATTITUDE. A vertical position of the body in which one leg is raised with a bent knee supported by the other leg which is either straight or in *demi-plié* position. Both the supporting and working legs should be turned out from the hip, although some contemporary movements permit the rotation to be turned in. The knee must be higher than the foot on the raised leg to achieve the proper image of an *attitude* and to develop the muscles properly. When working to hold the leg in its correct position, it is important to use the muscles in the thigh, and not the back muscles. One should not sickle (curve) the foot to give the appearance of the proper position, for besides being improper technique, it can cause tendonitis or lead to *plantar fasciitis*.

BALANCÉ. A movement done in waltz tempo in which the dancer shifts weight from one foot to the other. The transfers of weight are important and the dancer must make sure the ball of the foot bears the weight when the foot touches in back. However, the weight must be evenly dispersed through the foot when the whole foot touches the floor.

BALLONNÉ. A springing movement executed by jumping into the air while extending the other leg from the knee or ankle and then returning it to the same spot when the supporting leg lands back on the floor. This movement begins and ends with the body supported by one leg; therefore, it is necessary to be pulled-up and centrally balanced in the upper torso. The weight cannot fall back into the heel because such action will inhibit the springing motion required to do a *ballonné*.

BALLOTTÉ. Also referred to as *jeté bateau*, this is a jumping movement often accompanied by a swaying motion of the body. In order to avoid the risk of injury, the weight of the body must be centered so that the slight lean of the body will not pull it off balance. It is also necessary to be pulled-up in the upper torso so that the springing off the floor will not require extra effort from the feet, which could strain the muscles.

CABRIOLE. A jumping movement in which one leg is raised and the supporting leg springs upward and outward to beat the raised leg, thus giving the illusion of pushing the working leg higher, and then landing on the supporting leg. As with any jumping movement, even weight distribution must be maintained to avoid undue pressure on the supporting foot. Also, it is important to control the body from the abdominal muscles to take the pressure off the muscles of the lower extremity. When the abdominal muscles are not used, the force into the knee can be great and a twisting motion will lead to specific injury.

DÉVELOPPÉ. A developing movement done by standing on one leg and bringing the other foot up from the ankle to the knee of the standing leg and then stretching, or developing, the leg to its fullest. It is important to be centered over the ball of the foot and stay in alignment while executing this movement. Also, an effort must be made not to allow the supporting foot to roll in or out to avoid any muscle or ligament strain.

ÉCHAPPÉ. A springing movement in which the feet spring out simultaneously to second or fourth position. Proper placement of the feet on the floor is essential to this movement so that the dancer can check for correct positioning after the springing action. It is important not to roll in

Debora Chase and Ralph Glenmore of the Alvin Ailey American Dance Center demonstrate elevation in Stack-up by Talley Beatty. Photo by Marbeth.

or out in order to avoid stress on the feet. The ball of the foot is receiving a great impact on landing. This can cause *periostitis*, bursitis, *capsulitis*, and *sesamoiditis*. The heel should always touch the ground on landing; otherwise, shinsplints will occur. Being pulled-up in the upper torso is also necessary to achieve a good balance.

ÉLÉVATION. A descriptive term referring to the height attained in a jump. A strong Achilles tendon provides the spring for high *élévation;* the elasticity of the tendon can be increased through all forms of *demi-plié*, with the heels remaining firmly on the ground. It is necessary to control placement to avoid undue strain on the feet during takeoff and landing.

ENTRECHAT. An elevation step in which a dancer jumps straight up in the air and crosses the feet, beating the calves against each other and changing the feet. It is important to be lifted from the center, with the shoulders squarely over the hips, to do an *entrechat*. A good *plié* with proper turnout is also essential to ensure a solid takeoff with the feet. While in the air, the body should remain erect and the toes should be pointed.

ÉTENDRE. One of the basic principles of dance, which is to stretch. When stretching the feet, it is important to allow them to move freely without gripping or tightening the muscles. Such action can cause the arches to cramp and can result in an injury if the arches aren't treated properly.

FOUETTÉ. A movement involving a whipping action of the working leg and upper body. It is important to be securely pulled up out of the hips so as not to cause undue pressure on the legs and feet. While the whipping action is being done it is necessary to use the abdominals and stay centered to ensure a smooth transition on the supporting leg and a safe landing on the foot.

GLISSADE. A gliding movement that is usually done prior to jumps requiring high elevation. It is necessary to be pulled up from the abdominals and turned out in fifth position *plié* so the supporting foot can provide a strong spring for the leg and body. If the foot is required to accommodate for incorrect body weight distribution and inadequate turnout, it may be injured in the process of doing a *glissade*.

JETÉ. A jumping step in which the weight is transferred from one foot to the other and executed with a throwing motion of the leg. As is important with all jumps, the dancer must be centered to insure a good springoff from the supporting leg. The higher the elevation, the less the risk of

Portia Poindexter and Junius Backus of Alvin Ailey American Dance Center perform jetés in Connotations: Brazil *by Walter Raines. Photo by Marbeth.*

injury upon landing, as the dancer will have sufficient time to properly point the foot in air and then place it correctly on the floor.

PAS DE BASQUE. A step derived from Basque folk dancing done in three movements. It is important to be pulled-up from the hips so that the weight is not sitting on the heels of the feet. This will enable the dancer to spring up easier and will prevent unnecessary stress on the muscles in the feet, thus avoiding injury.

PIROUETTE. A turn of the body on one foot. First and foremost, the dancer must have the weight of the body properly distributed through both feet. Secondly, it is imperative that the knee of the supporting leg remain straight while turning. If it is not, the alignment of the body will be disturbed, causing the weight to shift, which can cause an injury to the foot. Also, it is necessary to spot while turning, which helps the dancer turn more easily and prevents stress to the legs and upper body.

PLIÉ. A bending movement of the knees with the legs rotated outward from the hip joints. While executing a *demi-plié* or *grand-plié*, the feet must stay comfortably on the floor, without tension in the toes. The feet should never be turned out to a greater degree than the knees or ankles.

Relevé in full pointe.

It is important not to allow the feet to roll in or out. Doing so will put added strain on the muscles, which could result in an injury. Rolling in or out also creates stress on the knees and could cause injury to them as well.

RELEVÉ. A movement that is performed by raising the body to *demi-pointe* or full *pointe*. The dancer must be centered over the hips and balls of the feet. It is important to be pulled-up through both the hips and upper torso. If the dancer's weight is not evenly distributed, extra stress will be placed on the feet when attempting to rise. This will create an opportunity for injury. The turnout must be controlled from the tops of the thighs as well as the ankles. When in *relevé,* the ankles must not wobble during the ascent or descent, nor while balancing in the *relevé* position. Wobbly ankles can endanger the metatarsal heads and cause pain in that region. Specific injuries include *sesamoiditis,* bursitis, *capsulitis, periostitis,* and *neuritis* or *neuralgia.* Care should be taken on the descent to make sure the weight does not shift to the heels unevenly as they return to the floor.

SAUTÉ. A jumping movement which starts and finishes in *demi-plié.* As with all jumps, the dancer must be pulled-up in the abdominals to relieve any stress in the legs and feet and keep the weight evenly distributed. Proper turnout is essential to avoid any injury to the knees and feet while springing upward or during the landing.

SISSONE. A jump from two feet to one foot. As with all jumping movements which require elevation, the dancer must be pulled-up in the upper torso and the weight must be centered over both legs prior to executing this movement. Because the landing is only on one foot, if the body weight is not properly distributed, the extra pressure could cause injury to the supporting foot.

TENDU. A movement in which one leg slides out to an extended, pointed position and then returns to the closed position. The supporting leg must remain straight and properly placed on the floor, without rolling in or out, or gripping the floor with the toes and with the weight evenly distributed. When the dancer slides the foot outward it is important not to raise the hip or move it out of alignment to insure proper stretch and strengthening of the muscles.

Ana Marie Forsythe teaching the Horton Class at Alvin Ailey American Dance Center. Photo by Marbeth.

Four

PREVENTATIVE CARE FOR FEET

REST AND NUTRITION

A dancer can control many aspects of his or her personal and dance habits to reduce the risk of injury. Fatigue, for example, is one condition a dancer should try to avoid. When the body fatigues, the chance for injury increases greatly. The body reaches a plateau after which continued exertion is counterproductive. A dancer should be disciplined enough to stop when this upper limit is reached.

To distinguish the time when fatigue sets in, a dancer should recognize the signs of overwork. One will experience a persistent soreness and stiffness in the muscles, joints, and tendons, or may feel as if the lower extremities are too heavy to lift. The dancer can experience frequent headaches, loss of appetite, sluggishness, absence of menstruation, and an actual drop in performance ability. Emotional responses also can point to fatigue. They include a loss of interest in dance class and performing, nervousness, depression, and an inability to relax. The end result of overwork will be dancing at a level much lower than the dancer's normal abilities.

Poor nutrition and vitamin or mineral deficiency can contribute to fatigue. Medications and drugs can also cause the same problems. For example, amphetamines do not retard or reduce fatigue—they only reduce the feeling of fatigue and mask the pain. Great damage can be done to the body in these cases.

Fatigue can lead to many injuries, among them shinsplints, stress fractures, sprains, and overuse compartment syndrome. Increasing your muscle flexibility and strengthening exercises can prevent acute reactions to overstress. Rest the area involved as soon as signs of fatigue are present. Apply ice to the painful area for ten to fifteen minutes. Compression and elevation are also helpful treatments. But again, the most effective treatment for an overuse injury is rest.

Most fatigue and overuse injuries occur to the novice and beginning dancer who have not developed adequate muscle coordination and stamina. Professionals, however, also are susceptible to these injuries. I recently treated a dancer from a New York ballet company who was unhappy with the height of his jumps. He spent one entire afternoon practicing jumps. Instead of stopping when the area started to hurt, he continued. The constant pressure of the repetitive force caused fatigue to his metatarsal area. He developed a stress fracture of his second *metatarsal* and missed four weeks of dancing. This illustration underscores how vital it is that you do not allow overuse and fatigue to cause a more serious injury.

STRETCHING

Stretching enables a dancer to maintain a flexible body. As a prevention to possible injury, stretching is probably the most important step a dancer can take. It has been estimated that 75 percent of all overuse syndrome injuries can be avoided with proper flexibility training.

Your feet are not independent parts of your body. They are connected to the body and are affected by it. You do not want to increase the flexibility of just your feet, but the flexibility of your entire body. The more limber any part of the whole becomes, the less chance an injury will occur.

For example, a tight hamstring muscle will cause additional strain on the calves. This strain could then cause a compensation of movement that affects your ankle. With repeated force to this area, ankle pain develops. Proper stretching and flexibility training of the entire body with an emphasis on the hamstrings can prevent the ankle pain. Warm up all muscles before dancing.

Stretching should be done before and after dancing. If there is a break in the middle of your session, it would be a good idea to stretch

Donna Wood and the members of the Alvin Ailey American Dance Center demonstrate the importance of flexibility. They are performing Divining *by Judith Jamison. Photo by Marbeth.*

again. It is important to develop a stretching routine that is suited to your body and its special needs.

The "no pain no gain" philosophy does not apply to stretching. Stretching should not produce any strain or pain. Stretch within your own limits; there should be no competition to outstretch another dancer.

A normal stretch should last about one minute. The first 20 to 30 seconds should be an easy stretch. Relax totally and feel the easy stretch. Then, slowly start to intensify the stretch and hold it for an additional 30 seconds. You should not feel pain or excessive strain. If you are overdoing the stretch, injury might occur. Remember, stretching is done to *avoid* injury and increase flexibility. Gradually, release the stretch.

Breathing should remain under control, slow, and in rhythm. Do not hold your breath. Do not make abrupt changes. Every movement should be gradual and slow. Bouncing or jumping can be harmful to the muscles.

With time, the feeling of the stretch changes and more time is needed to accomplish the desired effects. If one starts out very tight,

Keeping the legs straight, bend over hanging from the hips. Do this stretch first and repeat as the final stretch.

Knees are bent; the back is straight.

Do not sit on the ground. Keep yourself a few inches off the floor.

The back and supporting leg are straight. Repeat for the other leg.

Supporting leg is straight. Repeat for the other leg.

Lower extremity stretches for increased flexibility. Photos by Patrick Watson, courtesy of the Dance Studio, Vassar College.

Try to keep both legs straight. Repeat for the other leg.

The back, head, neck, and back leg are straight. The back foot can be held in three different positions: straight forward, 45° inward, or 45° outward. Repeat for the other leg.

46

Do not bend the extended leg that you are holding. Repeat for the other leg.

Same as the previous stretch except back knee is slightly bent. Repeat for the other leg.

Push your knees toward the ground and try to keep your back straight.

The front leg should be straight. Repeat for the other leg.

Keep both legs straight and on the ground.

Keep your body flat to the floor with your arm extended. Repeat for the other side.

Keep your body flat to the floor with your head resting on your arm. Repeat for the other leg.

Keep your body flat to the floor with your arm stretched on the floor. Repeat for the other leg.

modify the time of stretch accordingly. Instead of a total of 60 seconds, start with 30. After a few weeks, increase to 40, then 50 seconds. Time is not the important factor. How the stretch feels is more important and should control the time factor. Work within your own comfortable and strain-free limits. Days when you are extra tight will require a longer stretch time. Your body will determine the correct time needed for a proper stretch.

FOOT EXERCISES

It is to your advantage to have strong and healthy feet. For some dancers, additional foot exercises are helpful. Adding these exercises to your routine might prevent an injury from occurring.

Six simple exercises to strengthen your feet can be done every day. It should take no more than a few minutes. These are basically kinetic (moving) exercises. Isometric (pushing against a non-movable object) exercises can also be done. All of the following exercises should be done barefoot.

1. Gently curl your toes under while flexing your arch. You are trying to form the letter C with your foot. Hold this position for about 10 seconds, then relax. Switch feet and repeat this arch strengthening exercise.

2. While walking, rise on your toes and hold your weight for about two seconds. Then transfer your weight to the other foot and hold yourself up for another two seconds. Do this activity for a minute or two.

3. Curl your toes while you are sitting. Push your feet firmly against the floor. Your arches should start to rise. Hold this position for about five to 10 seconds and repeat it several times.

4. Put your weight on the toes of one foot. The nonweight-bearing foot should be put on top of the foot on the ground. Try to raise the bottom foot. At the same time, push down with the top foot. Hold this position for about five seconds. Switch feet and repeat the exercise.

5. Put a towel on the floor in front of your feet while you are sitting. try to pick up the towel using one foot at a time. Switch feet and repeat the exercise.

Mindy is a twenty-three-year-old woman with a major dance company. For more than two years, she had pain in the anterior aspect of her ankle on both feet. The discomfort varied in intensity but never caused her to miss a performance. Still, the problem was becoming chronic. Her problems intensified the longer she danced. She was starting to develop anterior shinsplints.

Nothing abnormal appeared on her X-rays. Palpation revealed no tenderness or pain. One problem did surface during Mindy's biomechanical exam. Due to an extremely tight posterior muscle group, she had an equinus condition. Athletes commonly overdevelop their posterior leg muscles, causing them to tighten. Mindy had developed an overuse syndrome with compensation occurring at the anterior aspect of her ankles.

I started her on a rigid program of stretching. Mindy was spending at least one hour every day stretching the area. By increasing her flexibility and stretching the posterior muscles, her symptoms began to subside within a few weeks.

After only two weeks, she was amazed at how much deeper she could bend when performing a *plié*. She believed she was getting a better pushoff on her jumps. Within a few months, her symptoms disappeared. No more shinsplints or ankle pain. Stretching was now a vital part of her routine life.

6. With the towel still in front of your feet, keep your heels on the ground. Using the front of your foot, try to push the towel to the side. Then try to push the towel to the other side. Repeat with your other foot.

These simple exercises can be done anywhere and repeated several times a day. The normal activities dancers do in every class will help strengthen their feet and lower extremities. An example of this is the *demi-plié*. Each time it is done, one strengthens the arch and the plantar muscles of the foot. *Relevés* strengthen the toes, ball of the foot, and posterior muscles of the lower extremities. To avoid injury, again remember the importance of flexibility stretching by warming up and cooling down.

MASSAGE

Massage also can be a very valuable addition to a treatment plan. For aching and tired feet, massage can help relieve stress and strain. It can also be used as a therapy for certain inflammatory conditions. Your doctor might send you to a massage therapist as treatment.

For general foot massage, follow these directions. Massage after applying heat to your feet. The best time is after a hot bath. Rest one foot across your other knee. Massage your foot in a circular motion using the heel of your hand. Start at the toes and work your way back. Bend each toe separately in each direction and gently rotate each toe. Tug at the toe very carefully. Move up along the sole and sides of your foot. Knead the arch area using your thumbs. Then repeat the massage for the other foot.

FOOT HYGIENE

Proper hygiene is an important form of preventative medicine. Many problems or potential injuries can be avoided if the dancer maintains his or her feet and legs. The adage, "An ounce of prevention is worth a pound of cure" is true. Follow these basic suggestions:

- Wash and dry your feet daily. Apply powder after you dry your feet. Pay particular attention to the areas between your toes.

- Trim toenails to a slightly rounded edge. Do not cut into the corners of the nails. Use a nail clipper or other proper instrument.

- Wear natural fiber socks (cotton, wool) and change them daily. They will absorb perspiration, allow your feet to breathe, and reduce bacteria that can cause foot odor.

- Smooth hard, rough skin with a pumice stone after bathing to soften your feet. Apply a moisturizer to the skin. A certain layer of hard skin is necessary for some dancers, but do not allow the skin to thicken too much or it will cause pain and pressure. Let your podiatrist remove excessive calluses or corns.

- Make sure your shoes are comfortable and fit correctly. Improper and ill-fitting shoegear can cause tremendous damage.

- Use a hand cream or lotion on your feet at night. This should prevent dryness and the possibility of fissures developing.

- Avoid excesses of exposure to hot and cold. Wear warm socks and shoes or boots during the winter months. Do not allow your feet to sunburn.

- Smoking (nicotine) and caffeine can reduce the circulation to your feet. Try to avoid excesses of both.

- Avoid home surgery for corns and calluses, and do not use sharp instruments or strong chemicals on your feet for any reason.

Yvonne Hall performing for Dance Theatre of Harlem. Photo by Marbeth.

Five

MEDICAL
TREATMENT

WHEN TO SEE A DOCTOR

Dancers dread injury and fear doctors who might tell them they should never dance again. For this reason many dancers do not seek proper medical attention.

Dancers must make two decisions when a medical problem arises: Should I see a doctor for this problem?, and if so, who is the best doctor to see? The decision to see a doctor or treat the problem yourself is difficult. Not only fear but financial considerations as well enter the picture. Availability and convenience of making appointments with additional loss of dance time also enters into the decision-making process.

Medical problems and injuries can be divided into three categories: mild, moderate, and severe. Placing your medical problem into one of these categories will help you decide whether it is time to see a specialist.

Severe injuries or medical problems render decision making unnecessary. There is no decision; medial attention is a must. Severe problems can be defined as those that stop you from dancing. If you cannot dance because the pain is too great, immediate and proper treatment is vital. Pain is your body's signal that something is wrong.

At the other extreme are problems in the mild category. These are injuries and medical problems that do not stop you from dancing or interfere with your performance. They are just annoying. In most instances you can treat these conditions yourself. Follow the advice given in a first-aid or health book. Speak to a dance instructor or fellow dancer. Most mild injuries or medical problems will improve in just a few days. If they are not getting better, or even becoming worse, it is time for professional help.

Moderate injuries are the hardest to determine appropriate treatment for. Moderate problems cause discomfort and interfere with your skills. You can still dance, but not at your normal level of performance.

Unfortunately, there are times when proper medical attention should have been sought for a moderate injury but was not. With a delay in receiving adequate care, the problem can worsen. A relatively minor problem can turn into a chronic condition. Do not delay professional care if your own treatment has not brought about improvement within the first 24 hours.

Some professionals specialize in the treatment of dancers. Doctors who treat dancers know the questions to ask and how dancing will affect specific areas of the body. They will try to keep you dancing even when injured, if at all possible. The best way to find this type of doctor is to ask fellow dancers, instructors, or any person involved with the dance world. Not only will a doctor trained to treat dancers keep you dancing whenever possible, he or she can also get you back to full performance faster than physicians who do not know the intricacies of dance. Second opinions are also important. Sometimes a different approach to your problem can get you back dancing sooner.

HISTORY AND EXAMINATION

Most dancers will experience a foot problem that requires medical attention during their careers. It could be an injury, or pain might develop from a medical problem. Whether the problem is acute or chronic, a doctor should be thorough when treating a dancer.

HISTORY

The first thing a doctor should do is take a dancer's complete history. A good history is invaluable in diagnosing the origin of a dancer's complaint. Using an accurate and thorough history, the doctor is able to take each specific complaint and direct it toward a differential diagnosis.

First, you must describe your chief complaint. Be sure to include all the specific details you can. How long have you had the problem? Has it been getting better or worse? Does it bother you more in the morning?

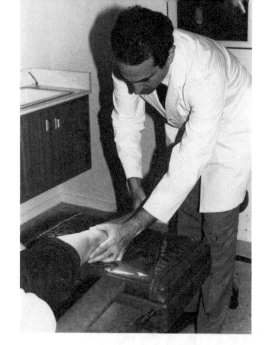

Dr. Spilken puts the foot through a range of motion during the physical examination. Photo by Eric Shonz.

Dr. Spilken examines the forces affecting the foot during relevé and demi-plié. Photo by Eric Shonz.

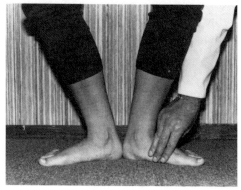

How does dancing affect the problem? It might be a good idea to write everything down before going to the office. Be sure to include all previous treatments. That includes what you have done, and what other professional care has been rendered. It will help the doctor to know what has worked and what has not.

The doctor should also ask you about your general health. Other medical problems can be related to foot problems. Doctors who merely look at your foot without considering your overall health status might miss the bigger picture that is causing the problem. This part of the history should include previous operations, medications you are taking, whether you are under a physician's treatment, and a brief family history when relevant. Let the physician know if you are allergic to any medications. Your dance history is also vital to establishing a diagnosis and a treatment plan.

EXAMINATION

The examination should include palpation and movement of both feet. Palpation is the method of examining the surface of the body by laying the flat of the hand upon the skin. Even if the problem involves only one foot both feet should be checked. A careful description of swelling, lesions, or limitations of motion should be made.

A biomechanical examination and gait analysis usually should be performed. Watching the patient walk is extremely important. A patient's gait is usually an indication of where forces are acting and compensation is taking place. A good biomechanical exam and gait analysis could pick up a minor problem that is being multiplied by a dancer's activity. X-rays might also be necessary for a proper diagnosis. X-rays not only show fractures but also abnormal forces that might contribute to the problem. Other tests might be necessary, including cultures, blood or urine exams, or more sophisticated tests.

PADDINGS AND STRAPPINGS

One of the primary treatments for almost all dance injuries is the proper use of paddings and strappings. Eliminating weight bearing and redistributing body weight allows for faster healing. Numerous principles should be followed to make padding and strapping effective. No matter how scientific the construction, if these principles are not considered, the results might be more annoying to you than the original complaint. The following principles are essential to your comfort.

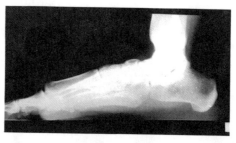

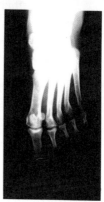

X-rays showing different views of the foot. Proper positioning of the foot with the correct angles is vital to allow the physician to determine any possible pathology.

1. The correct thickness of pad must be used. A pad that is too thin will not accomplish its primary function. A too-thick pad could cause constriction or pressure between the shoe and the foot.

2. The correct size and shape of material must be used. This is dependent on the location being treated and type of function that is desired. If the size and shape are not correctly measured, the symptoms might not be relieved and more discomfort might ensue. No part of the material should impinge upon any area of irritation or inflammation.

3. If an aperture is necessary, it must have the proper shape. Too small an opening can put pressure directly into the area from which you want to alleviate the forces. Too big an aperture means that normal weight bearing or pressure will exist. Apertures should be circular or oval and just slightly larger than the lesion.

4. The pads must be properly thinned so pressure is evenly distributed and high points avoided. Pressure must be distributed away from the area being protected.

5. The pad must be put on the skin in the correct manner, using adherents when necessary. This could avoid slippage and possible irritation from the pad.

6. Strapping should be applied with the correct amount of pressure. If the strapping is too tight the circulation might be constricted and necessary expansion of the tissue prevented. If it is too loose no therapeutic effects will be gained. A strapping that completely encircles a toe might compromise the circulation to that part.

7. The skin should not be puckered or pulled into folds by excessive tension. Air gaps should not be left between the material and the skin.

8. Joints should not be inadvertently immobilized. Undesired restriction of a joint's range of motion might ensue needlessly and cause added problems.

9. When using skin adherents, never apply them onto the lesion itself. Always permit the adherent to dry thoroughly before applying the pad.

10. Paraffin applied over the finished pad or tape will prevent the material from sticking to the stockings or shoes. It will also give the material some degree of resistance to water.

Problems also can develop with the incorrect use of padding and strapping techniques. The following can be the cause of failure of one of these modes of treatment.

1. Incorrect size or shape of material used. This will defeat the purpose of a well-planned therapy. Each padding or strapping should remain in the correct boundaries as described for each technique. Plantar pads should cover as much area as possible to distribute weight bearing and avoid concentrations in one particular area.

2. Incorrect density, either too firm or too soft, to accomplish any correction. Too much bulk could cause pressure of the shoe against the foot.

3. Incorrect placement on the foot or leg. The therapy is of no value unless it is positioned over the correct anatomical area. Otherwise, nearby tissue (such as an adjacent toe) could cause irritation of that part.

4. A dance shoe that does not allow the pad or strap to function. It is essential to evaluate the type of shoe gear that you will be using.

5. Allergies to the materials used. You may develop contact dermatitis. Another problem may be maceration and a breakdown of the skin under the material.

The following list of paddings and strappings provides you with usage information and constructing techniques. Although the technical terms may be difficult at first, they are necessary for accuracy. Appendix I contains a complete guide to definitions that should be referred to should confusion arise.

Morton's Compensating Pad

PURPOSE

You would use Morton's Compensating Pad to alleviate symptomatic congenital short first metatarsal with a painful lesion under the second metatarsal head.

MATERIALS

1. ¼″ adhesive felt.

2. Soft lead marking pencil.

BOUNDARIES

The pad will extend distally on the medial side of the foot to fall approximately ¼″ distal to the first *metatarsal* head. The remaining anterior border will fall just proximal to the *metatarsal* heads. The posterior aspect of the pad will cross the foot at the first *metatarsal cuneiform articulation.*

CONSTRUCTION

1. Cut a piece of ¼″ felt into approximately a 3″ × 4″ rectangle.

2. Place the pad on the foot so that it covers all the *metatarsal* heads and is flush with the medial and lateral sides of the foot.

3. With a soft lead pencil draw a line from just behind the fifth *metatarsal* head diagonally across the foot just behind the *metatarsal* heads to a point between the first and second *metatarsal* heads. From here the line continues distally between the first and second *metatarsal* heads to a point at the distal aspect of the first *metatarsal* head. The line is then carried in a medial direction to the medial border of the first *metatarsal*. The line then passes proximally following the contour of the first *metatarsal* shaft and changes direction to cross the foot in a lateral direction at the first *metatarsal cuneiform articulation*. The line is finished by continuing to the starting point by following the lateral border of the fifth *metatarsal* shaft proximally.

ADDITIONAL COMMENTS

The pad can be easily secured for longer wear by adhering strips of 1″ adhesive tape across the plantar aspect of the foot at various points.

The Long Arch Pad

PURPOSE

This pad is used for long arch fatigue, symptomatic flat feet, ankle pain, foot strain, plantar fasciitis, or any pronatory problems.

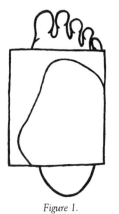

MATERIALS

1. ¼″ adhesive felt.

2. Soft lead pencil.

3. Spray adhesive.

Figure 1.

BOUNDARIES

Figure 2.

The pad follows the fourth intermetatarsal space laterally. The back edge crosses the foot anterior to the weight-bearing tuberosity of the *calcaneus*, the anterior edge passes proximal to the *metatarsal parabola* and the medial border passes proximally along the first *metatarsal* shaft to the first *metatarsal cuneiform articulation* where it slopes superiorly to the *talonavicular articulation*. The pad then passes immediately below the medial border of the heel.

CONSTRUCTION

1. Cut a rectangle from ¼" adhesive felt approximately 3½" × 6".

2. Lightly adhere the felt to the foot so that the lateral side of the foot is flush with a 6" edge of felt and the posterior edge rests just proximal to the weight-bearing tuberosity of the *calcaneus* (Fig. 1).

3. Now with a soft led pencil mark the shape of the pad by drawing a line just proximal to the *metatarsal parabola* to a point just between the first and second *metatarsal* heads. At this point the line is carried back along the plantar surface of the first *metatarsal* shaft to the *metatarsal cuneiform articulation* and then immediately below to the medial border of the heel.

4. Prepare the foot with spray adhesive and adhere pad (Fig. 2).

The Metatarsal Pad

PURPOSE

The *metatarsal* pad is used to relieve pressure from painful lesions located at the *metatarsal* heads.

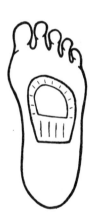

MATERIALS

1. ¼" adhesive felt.

2. Soft lead pencil.

3. Adhesive tape or moleskin.

BOUNDARIES

The anterior border follows the *metatarsal parabola* from a point just proximal to the *metatarsal* heads. The medial and lateral sides follow the first and fourth interspaces proximally to cross the foot perpendicular to the *metatarsals* at their bases.

CONSTRUCTION

1. Cut a piece of ¼″ felt 3″ × 4″.

2. Mark the felt pad according to the outline described in the boundary section above.

3. Adhere the pad to the foot.

4. Secure with adhesive tape or moleskin.

ADDITIONAL COMMENTS

This pad can be constructed to almost any need.

1. It may be extended forward either full thickness or with a long bevel to cover the three middle *metatarsal* heads. This variation can include a circular aperture to disperse weight away from a particular lesion.

2. The pad can also be constructed as a single or double wing shape isolating the first or fifth *metatarsal* heads or both with a full width metatarsal pad going completely across the foot.

3. The *metatarsal* pad can be incorporated into other pads for the plantar surfaces of the foot.

4. The pads can be strapped with adhesive tape encircling the foot just proximal to the *metatarsal* heads.

Parallel Strip Padding

PURPOSE

Parallel strip padding distributes weight and pressure away from painful lesions on the plantar surface of the foot.

MATERIALS

1. According to individual preference, adhesive felt of varying thickness can be used.

2. Moleskin.

BOUNDARIES

The pads are placed in parallel formation. The length and width of the pad is determined by the area to be protected.

CONSTRUCTION

1. Locate the lesion to be protected and by palpation determine the thickness of the pad to be used. Don't use more padding than necessary.

2. Now cut two strips of adhesive felt of exactly the same rectangular shape and size. The finished rectangle should be long enough to extend at least ½" distal and proximal to the lesion. The width of the strip should be at least ½".

3. Align the two pads in parallel position by adhering them to the foot. The pads should buttress the lesion on both sides and lie with the long axis of the pad facing in an anterior-posterior direction.

4. Cover both parallel strips with a piece of moleskin that approximates the shape and size of a metatarsal pad.

Parallel Strip Padding

PURPOSE

The pads are used to protect inflamed tissue at any area of the first metatarsal phalangeal joint by diverting pressure away from the areas of irritation.

MATERIALS

¼", ⅛", or ³/₁₆" adhesive felt (according to depth of lesion).

BOUNDARIES

These pads will act as buttresses which will lie parallel to the lesion in question on its proximal and distal aspects.

CONSTRUCTION

1. Cut two rectangles of chosen thickness from the adhesive felt. The rectangles should be approximately 1" × 1½".

2. Now place one pad just proximal to the bunion. The long side of the pad will lie next to the lesion perpendicular to the long axis of the first *ray*.

3. The second pad is placed at the distal aspect of the bunion and parallel to the proximal pad.

The Dancer's Pad

PURPOSE

This pad is useful for symptomatic plantarflexed first *ray*, first *metatarsal* bursitis, *tibial*, or *fibular sesamoiditis*.

MATERIALS

1. ¼″ adhesive felt or adhesive foam.

2. Spray adhesive.

BOUNDARIES

The pad assumes the same shape and size of the metatarsal pad. However, the Dancer's Pad has an aperture at the medial, distal edge that begins distally between the first and second *metatarsal* heads and curves medially to meet the medial side of the pad approximately ⅝″ proximal to the first *metatarsal* head.

CONSTRUCTION

1. Construct a simple *metatarsal* pad from ¼″ adhesive foam or adhesive felt.

2. Cut an aperture in the pad to allow for weight distribution away from the first *metatarsal* head as described in the "boundaries" section.

3. Prepare the plantar surface of the foot with spray adhesive.

4. Adhere the pad in place with the distal end of the pad lying just proximal to the *metatarsal* head.

ADDITIONAL COMMENTS

1. The pad can be affixed to the plantar surface of the foot by binding it down with either moleskin, adhesive tape, or paper tape as indicated.

2. The aperture for this pad can also be placed on the lateral aspect of the pad to disperse weight away from the head of the fifth *metatarsal* as in the case of a painful tailor's bunion, or *hyperkeratotic lesion*.

Simple Nonremovable Bunion Shield

PURPOSE

The shield is used for painful protrusion or bursitis on the medial or dorsal aspect of the first *metatarsal phalangeal* joint.

MATERIALS

1. ¼″ or ⅛″ adhesive foam or adhesive felt.

2. Moleskin.

BOUNDARIES

The pad will encircle one half the proximal aspect of the protrusion and extend proximally on the medial aspect off the foot approximately 1 to 1 ½″.

CONSTRUCTION

1. Scissor cut a piece of adhesive foam or felt into a rectangle 1″ × 1½″ (the depth of the material should be at the same level as the protrusion when placed on the skin).

2. Cut a semicircular crescent into the felt at one end that approximates the outer border of the protrusion.

3. Taper the opposite end of the felt with scissors so it assumes the shape of half an oval.

4. Adhere the pad to the skin with the oval end facing proximally on the medial aspect of the first *metatarsal*.

5. Fashion a piece of moleskin approximating the shape of the pad allowing ¼″ overlap on all borders and adhere directly to the pad.

ADDITIONAL COMMENTS

The pad can be fashioned to accommodate any lesion on the medial or lateral side of the foot.

"T" Sling For Hallux Valgus

PURPOSE

The "T" sling removes pressure from a painful second toe that is being caused by a flexible *hallux valgus* deformity.

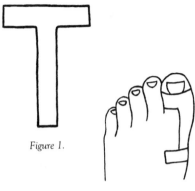

Figure 1.

MATERIALS

1. 3" moleskin.

Figure 2.

BOUNDARIES

The moleskin will encircle the base of the *hallux* and extend proximally where it is secured on the medial aspect of the first *metatarsal* shaft.

CONSTRUCTION

1. Using sharp straight scissors, cut the 3" moleskin into a "T" shape so that the horizontal bar of the "T" is 1" wide by 2½" long and the vertical bar of the "T" is 1" wide by 4" long (Fig. 1).

2. Prepare the first *metatarsal* and *hallux* by spraying with adhesive.

3. Wrap the 2½" horizontal bar around the base of the *hallux* leaving the vertical bar directly over the medial aspect of the first *metatarsal phalangeal* joint. The vertical bar will point in a proximal direction.

4. Now passively adduct the *hallux* until it is articulating with the first *metatarsal* head and the *valgus* deformity is corrected.

5. While holding the great toe in corrected position, adhere the vertical member of the "T" tightly to the medial aspect of the first *metatarsal* head and shaft.

6. Secure the vertical bar with 1" adhesive tape where necessary (Fig. 2).

ADDITIONAL COMMENTS

This strapping can also be used on the lateral side of the foot to pull the 5th toe away from the 4th toe.

Aperture Pad or U-Pad For Lesser Toes

PURPOSE

Aperture pads relieve the symptoms of corns. U-pads relieve the
pressure on soft-tissue lesions or
corns.

MATERIALS

1. $^1/_{16}$", $^1/_8$", $^1/_4$", or $^1/_2$" adhesive
   or non-adhesive felt.

2. Chamois.

3. Moleskin.

4. Sponge rubber.

5. Rubber cement.

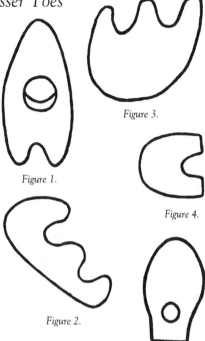

Figure 1.

Figure 2.

Figure 3.

Figure 4.

Figure 5.

BOUNDARIES

The pad is placed about the area in an attempt to distribute
pressure away from the lesion, bone, and joint involved.

CONSTRUCTION

1. Select an appropriate material of suitable thickness; do not make
   the pad too thick.

2. Cut the material to approximate the size of the entire area to be
   shielded.

3. Fold the material in half along its long axis (do not approximate
   the adhesive sides of any adhesive material).

4. Cut an aperture or U that will, when fitted, just surround the
   lesion; the pad should not touch the lesion or be too large; position
   the aperture in the center of the distal half of the material, insuring
   that the bulk of the padding will be proximal to the lesion (Fig. 1).

5. Trim the pad to the configuration that best fits the area around the
   lesion; shapes commonly utilized include oval, circular, tear-drop,
   horse-shoe, crescent, and others (Figs. 2-5).

6. Adhere pad to toe; use rubber cement if material is non-adhesive.

7. Bind pad to toe using Elastoplast, podiatry tape, Gaustex, lamb's wool, or other suitable material.

ADDITIONAL COMMENTS

A suitable medication can be applied to the lesion within the aperture and covered with a plug of sterile cotton before the padding is secured with a binding.

Sponge Rubber Heel Pad

PURPOSE

This heel pad is used to help relieve the symptoms of heel spur, *plantar fasciitis*, and *calcaneal periostitis*.

MATERIALS

½″ sponge rubber.

BOUNDARIES

The pad extends over the entire plantar aspect of the *calcaneus*.

CONSTRUCTION

1. Cut a rectange of ½″ sponge rubber that is as wide as the affected heel and as long as the distance from the proximal border of the heel to about midway in the longitudinal arch.

2. Round the proximal end of the rectangle to the contour of the heel.

3. Starting from the midpoint of the length of the rectangle, thin the rubber to a feather-edge distally.

4. Cut out a suitable aperture positioned at the site of the insertion of the *plantar fascia* to the *calcaneus*.

5. Place pad in heel of shoe or adhere to foot itself with suitable binding.

Gibney Ankle Strap (Basketweave)

PURPOSE

This ankle strap helps to prevent inversion and eversion of the ankle to occur while allowing plantar-flexion and dorsiflexion. Usage is primarily for ligamentous sprains and tendon injuries to prevent motion. This strapping is also very common before athletic competition to stabilize the ankle.

MATERIALS

1″ adhesive tape cut into strips. The size of each strip and the number needed is dependent on the size of the ankle.

BOUNDARIES

Runs on the medial and lateral side of the leg 5″ above the *malleoli*. It extends from the medial and lateral side of the foot just proximal to the first and fifth metatarsal heads.

CONSTRUCTION

1. Hold the ankle in its neutral position with the foot 90° to the leg or slightly plantarflexed.

2. Place the first piece of tape 5″ above the medial *malleolus* on the medial aspect of the leg near the Achilles tendon. Bring the strip under the heel and on the lateral side of the leg to 5″ above the lateral *malleolus*.

3. The second strip starts proximal to the 1st *metatarsal* head around the medial border of the foot, across the heel and extends just proximal to the head of the fifth *metatarsal*.

4. The next strip runs perpendicular and overlaps the first strip by ½″ and runs parallel to this strip.

5. The fourth strip runs horizontal and overlaps the second strip by ½″ and runs parallel to this strip.

6. Continue this pattern until the basketweave effect is achieved.

J-Strap

PURPOSE

The J-strap is used to prevent eversion of the *calcaneus*. It is used primarily for medial ligamentous injury following eversion sprains.

Figure 1.

MATERIALS

1½″ or 2″ adhesive strip.

BOUNDARIES

Extends from the lateral side of the foot just inferior to the lateral *malleolus* to the middle of the medial aspect of the leg.

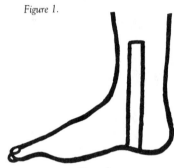

Figure 2.

CONSTRUCTION

1. Measure and cut a piece of tape to cover the boundaries indicated.

2. Place one end of the strip just inferior to the lateral *malleolus* on the lateral side of the foot (Fig. 1).

3. Exert pressure as the strap comes under the heel and onto the medial side of the leg about half-way up (Fig. 2).

ADDITIONAL COMMENTS

1″ adhesive tape anchors can be put over the ends of the strap to secure it in place.

Reverse "J"

PURPOSE

This strap accomplishes the opposite of the J-strap by limiting inversion of the *calcaneus*. It is used primarily for lateral ligamentous injury following inversion sprains.

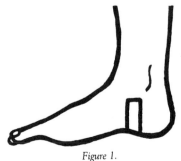

Figure 1.

MATERIALS

1½" or 2" adhesive tape strip.

BOUNDARIES

Extends from the medial side of the foot just inferior to the medial malleolus to the middle of the lateral side of the leg.

Figure 2.

CONSTRUCTION

1. Measure and cut a piece of tape to cover the boundaries indicated.

2. Place one end of the strip just inferior to the medial *malleolus* on the medial aspect of the heel (Fig. 1).

3. Apply tension as the tape is put under the heel and upwards on the lateral aspect of the leg about halfway up (Fig. 2).

ADDITIONAL COMMENTS

1" adhesive tape anchors can be put over the ends of the strap to secure it in place.

Heel Lock

PURPOSE

The heel lock is to be used for *plantar fasciitis* and associated heel spur syndrome. It also relieves pressure over the *talonavicular* joint.

Figure 1.

MATERIALS

1" adhesive tape.

BOUNDARIES

Extends from the lateral aspect just proximal to the 5th *metatarsal* head to the medial aspect just distal to the first *metatarsal* head.

CONSTRUCTION

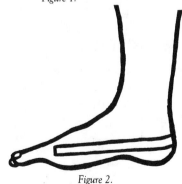

Figure 2.

1. Measure and cut one strip of 1" adhesive tape to fit the above boundaries.

2. Place one end on the lateral aspect of the foot just proximal to the 5th *metatarsal* head (Fig. 1).

3. Place the tape around the foot onto the medial side. The strip should end just distal to the 1st *metatarsal* head (Fig. 2).

ADDITIONAL COMMENTS

1. Usually used in conjunction with a Plantar Rest Strap.

2. Also used frequently with a longitudinal pad for the indications above.

Plantar Rest Strap (Campbell's)

PURPOSE

Campbell's strap is used to reduce strain and pressure on the plantar on the foot including the *plantar fascia.*

MATERIALS

1. Three or four strips of 1½" or 2" adhesive tape.

2. Two anchor strips of 1" adhesive tape.

BOUNDARIES

Runs from the lateral to medial sides of the foot covering the plantar aspect just beneath the *maleoli.*

CONSTRUCTION

1. Measure and cut four strips of 1½" or 2" adhesive tape to the desired length.

2. Apply the first strip on the lateral aspect of the foot just below the *malleoli.* Cross the plantar surface and attach the strip on the medial aspect to the top of the *navicular* (Figs. 1, 2).

3. The second strip is put on distal to the first and overlapping by one-third. It runs parallel to the first and maintains the same boundaries.

4. The third and fourth pieces are also put on distally and overlapping the preceding strip by one-third.

5. The strapping is finished with two horizontal anchors of 1" tape (Fig. 3).

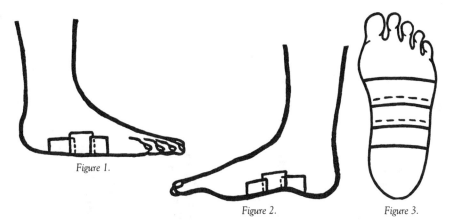

Figure 1.

Figure 2.

Figure 3.

ADDITIONAL COMMENTS

1. Usually used in conjunction with a longitudinal arch pad or other plantar padding.

2. A heel lock can be applied with this strapping to form a Low-Dye Strap.

3. Be especially careful not to wrinkle the skin while applying the tape.

4. Modifications to give additional support can be made. These modifications are then covered with the rest strap as described above. The modifications are:

    a. A two-inch strip is placed from the center of the heel posterior to the *substentaculum tali* and extends to the posterior of the *metatarsal* heads.

    b. Two one-inch strips run from the center of the heel to: (1) posterior of the first *metatarsal* head, and (2) posterior of the fifth *metatarsal* head.

Low-Dye Strap

PURPOSE

This strap is used to alleviate the strain associated with pronation. Primarily used for *plantar fasciitis*, heel spur syndrome and other symptoms caused by pronation at the *mid-tarsal* joint.

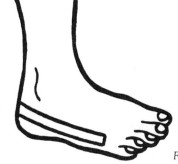

Figure 1.

MATERIALS

1. One strip of 1" adhesive tape.

2. Four strips of 1½" or 2" adhesive tape.

3. Two strips of 1" adhesive tape anchors.

BOUNDARIES

Same boundaries as indicated in the Heel Lock and the Plantar Rest Strap.

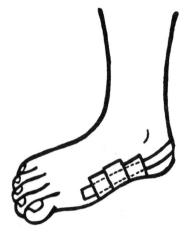

Figure 2.

CONSTRUCTION

1. Apply a Heel Lock as previously described. Before securing the tape on the medial aspect, adduct the forefoot slightly. This will hold the *hallux* towards the mid-line of the body (Fig. 1).

2. Over the Heel Lock apply a Plantar Rest Strap as previously applied including the horizontal anchors (Fig. 2).

ADDITIONAL COMMENTS

1. Paddings are usually used in conjunction with this strapping (e.g., Longitudinal Arch pad).

2. Bearing weight on the affected foot without wearing shoegear has a tendency to loosen this strapping.

Spica Toe Dressing

PURPOSE

This dressing immobilizes a digit after fracture or dislocation or following postoperative surgical procedures.

MATERIALS

Four to six strips of ⅛" or ¼" adhesive tape 3"—4" long.

BOUNDARIES

Covers the entire digit on all aspects.

CONSTRUCTION

1. Start the first strip on the dorsal medial aspect of the affected toe at its base. Extend the strip obliquely to the lateral aspect of the toe, across the plantar of the toe and obliquely back to the lateral aspect on the *dorsum* at the base of the toe.

2. The second strip attaches just lateral to the first strip and runs parallel to that strip.

3. Continue with overlapping strips until the entire toe is encircled with tape and properly immobilized.

ADDITIONAL COMMENTS

1. Obviously the tape is applied over the sterile dressing when used postoperatively.

2. It is extremely important to tape the toe in the correct position so that healing occurs in the desired position.

Campbell's Posterior Rest Strap

PURPOSE

This strap is used to alleviate strain from the Achilles tendon and support the posterior muscle group of the leg; also for Achilles tendonitis, *plantaris tendon rupture*, and *calcaneal apophysitis*.

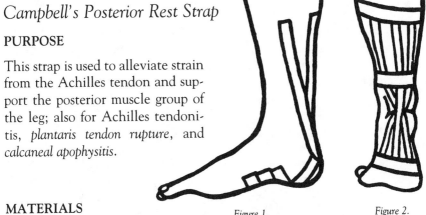

Figure 1.   Figure 2.

MATERIALS

1. Three strips of 1″ adhesive tape approximately 18″ long.

2. Three strips of 2″ adhesive tape 4″-6″ long.

BOUNDARIES

Extends from the plantar of the Lisfranc's joint up the back two-thirds of the lower leg.

CONSTRUCTION

1. Apply the first 18″ strip of tape starting at the plantar medial aspect of the foot inferior to the 1st *cuneiform*. Extend this piece obliquely towards the lateral aspect of the heel and up the lateral side of the lower leg.

2. Apply the second 18″ strip of tape starting at the plantar lateral aspect of the foot inferior to the base of the fifth *metatarsal*. Extend this piece obliquely toward the medial aspect of the heel and up the medial side of the lower leg (Fig. 1).

3. The third equal strip starts plantar to *Lisfranc's joint* in the center of the foot. Extend this strip posteriorly over the heel and up the center of the lower leg.

4. Apply the first 2″ anchor around the leg just superior to the ankle joint. The anchor strips are applied 90° to the original strips.

5. The last two 2″ anchors are applied at the ends of the 1″ tape (Fig. 2).

ADDITIONAL COMMENTS

1. A heel lift in the shoe is also effective in conjunction with this strapping.

2. The tape should be applied with the foot mildly plantarflexed. Applying tension while applying the 1″ strips will further plantarflex the foot.

ORTHOTIC DEVICES

Orthotics are custom-made supportive devices that can easily be moved from one type of shoe to another for various activities. The doctor takes a series of nonweight-bearing and weight-bearing measurements of the joints of the feet and legs. These may be related to X-ray studies. Then a cast (plaster model) is made of the foot in its neutral position (which is the position of maximum efficiency for the individual). From the resulting mold a orthotic laboratory produces a permanent cushion, supportive, or balancing device that corrects posture and provides resilient support. When done properly, this treatment corrects certain imbalance problems and prevents overuse stresses. In addition to orthotic devices, if the doctor

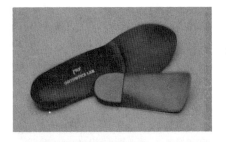

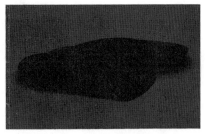

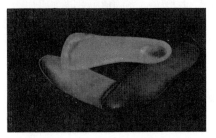

Orthotics can be made from soft or rigid materials. They can be cut to the metatarsal heads or full length. Your podiatrist will help determine which type of orthotics will best control your specific problems. Photos from FRS Orthotics Laboratory.

understands the biomechanics of the individual, injuries can be treated without loss of valuable training time.

Two problems that can be treated with orthotics are *pronation* and *hypermobility*. Pronation is the rolling inward of the forefoot. Hypermobility occurs when the motion in the joint is in excess of accepted limits for that joint.[1] While you may not be able to diagnose your particular problem, you should become aware that something is wrong when you experience a persistent strain, discomfort, or pain in your lower legs and feet when dancing. The pain could start in your spine and travel down through your hips, knees, and ankles, ending in your feet. This can occur because dancers perform complex motion in the hip and spine and their muscles require stability and strength to set and hold positions for long periods of time.[2] One way to help reduce the injury or strain that afflicts a dancer is through the use of orthotic devices.

After the manufacturing of your custom orthotics is completed, you will return to your doctor's office. There you will be fitted with your orthotic devices. During the break-in period, you may feel some discomfort. Wear the orthotics for one hour the first day, increasing wear time one hour each day. After approximately one week, you should be wearing them all day.

During the first few weeks wearing your orthotics, your feet and legs are changing to function more effectively. You may experience some unfamiliar feelings, including a slight pressure in your instep, a feeling of support in your arch, or an awareness of the outer edges. These feelings should disappear in a short time. If they do not, consult your podiatrist. A slight adjustment might have to be made. Your foot, orthotics, and shoe must function as a unit in order for you to function as a dancer.[3]

Proper training in flexibility and strength are obviously essential to preventing dance injury. Awareness of the total range of motion available and staying within this limit is also necessary to prevent excess stress from developing on body linkages. The use of proper orthotic devices can provide additional stability and support to minimize excessive stress to the feet, knees, and hips. In addition, they can provide protection for injured dancers to allow earlier return to activity.[4]

PHYSICAL THERAPY

Physical therapy can greatly aid the treatment of a dancer. Many injuries will heal more quickly when physical therapy is added to the treatment plan. The main purpose of this form of therapy is to reduce inflammation and swelling and to prevent the development of scar tissue.

Hydrotherapy is the most common form of physical therapy for the feet. Whirlpools produce a swirling action of water that massages and soothes the feet. The water temperature normally is between 100°F and 104°F. The effect of the heat and massage is to bring additional blood to the area. This helps in healing chronic injuries and should be used at least 24 to 48 hours after an injury. Cold water will help reduce the circulation and limit the immediate swelling that occurs after an injury. To be effective, hydrotherapy should be done several times a week.

Another important physical therapy modality for the lower extremity is the use of ultrasound. An ultrasound machine produces high-frequency sound waves that are absorbed into the deep tissue through the skin. The head of the machine is placed directly over the affected area. A transmitting gel is necessary to carry the sound waves from the machine to your body. Ultrasound helps speed healing and reduce swelling. It can help break up scar tissue formation. It is useful for injuries to ligaments, tendons, and muscles. To be effective, ultrasound should be applied several times a week.

Another form of physical therapy is paraffin (wax) foot baths. A patient dips a foot several times into the hot wax. A coating forms over the area dipped and a deep heating effect is created that lasts about ten minutes. Another treatment, galvanic stimulation, sends electrical impulses into the area through various conductors attached to the skin.

*J*oyce was a thirty-one-year-old modern dancer. To supplement her income, she also was a waitress. Over the past several months, she had developed arch pain. She admitted that she had been suffering from this problem for years, but during the last few months, it had gotten much worse. The pain increased greatly as the day progressed and after waiting tables.

A biomechanical examination and gait analysis revealed the cause of the problem. Joyce had a high-*cavus* foot type (a high arch). It was very flexible on weight bearing. Each step caused the high arch to stretch, flatten, and also roll inward. The foot was pronating excessively.

Her diagnosis was *plantar fasciitis*. The *fascia* band on the bottom of her feet became inflamed from the excessive movement. Walking and standing, not to mention dancing, would worsen the condition.

Immediate treatment consisted of padding and strapping each foot to minimize the stretch of the arch and decrease the pronatory forces. I also administered physical therapy and started her on an anti-inflammatory medication. She responded quickly to this treatment plan.

To control this condition over the long term, I had fabricated custom biomechanical orthotic devices. She had one pair for flat shoes and a dress orthotic made for her more fashionable shoes. With these orthotics, we were able to control the abnormal biomechanical forces that caused her arch pain. She felt immediate relief as the orthotics controlled the way her feet worked. She received control while waiting tables, walking, standing, and running. During jazz dance, she used her orthotics in her shoes. The only time she could not use the orthotics was when dancing barefoot. Joyce's symptoms disappeared and she has not had any pain since using the orthotics.

The electric current will stimulate the nerve endings and cause a twitching effect. Transcutaneous electronic nerve stimulation (TENS) units also have become very popular. TENS accomplish what galvanic machines do: they help in the healing process and minimize pain and discomfort.

It is important to receive proper physical therapy treatments. Too many treatments can cause damage; spaced too far apart, they become less effective. Using physical therapy for months sometimes can be a waste of effort and money. Usually, the beneficial effects of physical therapy are accomplished in just a few weeks. Not more than twelve treatments should ever really be necessary (four weeks of three treatments per week). Your physician might administer the physical therapy or send you to a trained physical therapist.

MEDICATION

Medications can be used as an adjunct to the therapy and treatment plan for many conditions. Medications should never be overused or taken without specific purposes, but when needed can help reduce inflammation, stop pain, and heal various problems.

Medications can be administered in many ways. The most popular forms are by mouth or through an injection. When taking medicines orally, follow the directions carefully. One pill three times a day does not mean taking three pills at bedtime. If you do not understand when or how to use a medicine, ask your doctor. Do not take it upon yourself to change the dosage. Some people think to themselves "If one pill helps, I might as well take two and get better twice as fast." But too much medicine can be harmful or even be toxic.

Medication by injection sends a drug directly into the area where it is needed. Most injections for dancers are to counter inflammation, the body's first reaction to injury. Injections can limit the amount of swelling and reduce the inflammatory process. Normally only a few injections are given for any inflammatory condition. They are usually given one week apart; you should not need more than three or four injections.

Virginia Johnson performing Othello *by John Butler for the Dance Theatre of Harlem. Dancers exert tremendous force on their feet and are very prone to injury. Photo by Marbeth.*

Six

DANCERS' FOOT PROBLEMS: A GLOSSARY

ABRASIONS

An *abrasion* is the actual scraping away of a portion of the skin layer (epidermis). This occurs primarily due to an abnormal mechanical movement causing rubbing. Barefoot dancers are more prone to this type of injury. As the foot slides or glides across the floor surface, it may stick. If the skin scrapes off, it can become very painful.

The reaction of the skin is similar to a burn. Precautions should be taken to prevent infection. The area should be antiseptically cleaned and an antibiotic or first-aid cream applied. The area should be protected with a sterile dressing while it heals. Proper padding and strapping techniques (See Chapter 5) are very helpful to reduce friction to the abraded area. Dancing may continue immediately depending upon the location of the injury and the presence of pain. Do not dance on the area if it causes increased pain. This will only delay the healing process.

APOPHYSITIS

Epiphyseal plates are the growth area of bones. If the growth area of a bone is traumatized, an inflammation occurs. This inflammation is called an *apophysitis*. In the dancer's foot, the most common area affected is the heel. The young dancer will experience pain in the back of the heel.

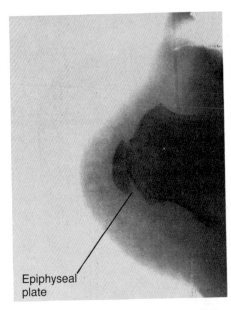

Polaroid X-ray showing the epiphyseal plate in the heel.

Epiphyseal
plate

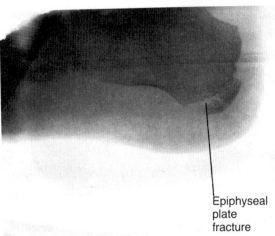

Epiphyseal
plate
fracture

The epiphyseal plate can fracture from excessive and repetitive forces as seen on this polaroid X-ray.

Apophysitis can occur only in young people who still are growing. It is one condition that can really be called "growing pain." It is most frequent between the ages of ten and fifteen and it affects boys more frequently then girls.

This condition is usually from repetitive trauma and results in a decrease in circulation to the affected area. It is worsened by jumps, turns, and a running motion. Any additional pressure on the affected area will cause a lot of pain and an inability to bear weight. While the heel is the most commonly affected area, any growth plate in a bone of a growing child can be affected.

Initial treatment is rest. Pressure must be taken off the area for three to four weeks. Ice can be used during the first 48 hours to reduce swelling. Anti-inflammatory medications might be needed for the discomfort. A heel lift about ¼″ to ½″ in height will reduce some of the pull of the Achilles tendon to relax the area (see Chapter 5). Apophysitis is usually fully healed in a month or two with full return to dance at that time.

ARTHRITIS

Arthritis by definition is a change in a joint. There are many different forms of arthritis actually describing 100 different diseases. They include *osteoarthritis, rheumatoid arthritis, psoriatic,* and *bacterial arthritis, gout,* and many others. Because each disease has its own treatment plan and prognosis, it is important to properly diagnose an arthritic condition. The most common arthritis for dancers is osteoarthritis or degenerative joint disease. As the name implies, excessive wear and tear breaks down the

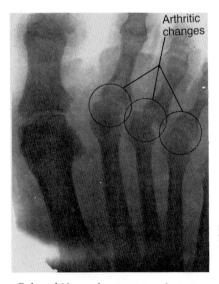

Polaroid X-ray showing joint changes at the second, third, and fourth metatarsal phalongeal joints.

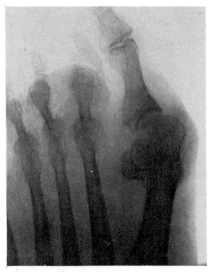

Severe arthritic changes in the left foot of this retired dancer as seen on a polaroid X-ray.

joint. This traumatic arthritis occurs from the excessive force a dancer generates on a specific joint. The force is greater than the joint's available range of motion. The condition can progressively worsen as the force continues over time. Pain is greatest after dance activity and stiffness can occur with inactivity. Joint motion can become limited. Obviously, a painful joint with a decreased range of motion will affect a dancer's performance greatly.

It is possible to develop arthritis secondarily. After a trauma, traumatic arthritis can form. The injury causes damage to the joint and it then forms arthritis. For this reason, sprains, strains, dislocations, fractures, and other injuries should be treated correctly.

Injection therapy with anti-inflammatories and anesthetics is very helpful. Physical therapy also can reduce swelling, limit scar tissue, and promote healing. Oral medications are sometimes necessary to limit inflammation and pain. Biomechanical orthotic devices are also very important. They will limit the abnormal motions causing strain on the involved joints, maximizing the efficiency of the joint and keeping it working in a neutral position. Surgery is sometimes necessary for joints that are constantly painful and have a limited range of motion. This should be performed only when all conservative measures have failed.

Treatment is needed to prevent arthritis from worsening. With good results, the condition is kept in check and further deterioration of the joint is prevented. Scar tissue formation can also be limited with prompt treatment. Arthritis cannot be cured but it can be made more manageable without disruption of dance time.

BLISTERS

Blisters are a separation of the outer layer of the skin, the epidermis, that fills with either a watery serous fluid or with blood. This is probably one of the most common problems for a dancer. As the blister develops, one feels a hot spot. If the pressure is removed from the area at this point, the blister will not form. As soon as you start to feel a hot spot on your foot, stop. A simple solution, such as a covering (bandage, moleskin) will reduce the friction and allow resumption of activity.

The most common causes of blisters are improperly fitting stockings, socks, or shoegear. This creates an area of friction from movement in the shoe or constant pressure from a tight fit. Sometimes the floor surface you are dancing on adds to the problem. The friction usually occurs in a twisting fashion, which disrupts the skin layers. Some people are prone to blisters because of the anatomical structure of their foot.

Blisters can be very painful. A raw layer of skin can be exposed and the fluid accumulation can put great pressure on the underlying tissues. Self-treatment should start with an antiseptic cleaning of the area. Puncturing the blister should only be done if there is pain. Sterilize a needle by holding it in a flame. Let it cool, then make a small puncture at the proximal-most border. Drain the fluid and leave the blistered skin intact. The skin acts as the best dressing to cover the area. Dispersion pads can be used to alleviate pressure from the immediate area. Dance can usually resume without any lost time. If treatment is not started right away, an infection might develop. Professional help should be sought if infection occurs. An infection might mean loss of several days of dancing.

Prevention is really more important than treatment. Make sure your dance shoes are the correct fit. Also, check for any problems with your stockings or socks. Perspiration can also add to the chance of blisters forming as moisture increases friction. Use powder and natural fiber socks to absorb any moisture.

For those who have a history of blisters in one area, applying petroleum jelly can reduce friction. Covering the area with a bandage, tape, or moleskin is also helpful. If blisters still occur, professional help is needed. Where biomechanics come into play, orthotics might be necessary. A pronating foot has an increased amount of friction and twisting. The orthotics will stop abnormal motions, and it is hoped, prevent chronic blistering.

BUNIONS

Bunions are an overgrowth of bone on the head of the first *metatarsal*. A bump will be seen and felt. The bump of bone can be very painful, especially in shoegear. On the outside of the foot, a tailor's bunion or bunionette can form. This appears at the head of the fifth *metatarsal*.

Inflammation from the rubbing of the bump can cause bursitis. It is also common to see the big toe pointing inward as the bunion progresses. A bunion easily leads to arthritis of the involved joint. That implies not only pain but a limitation of the range of motion of that joint. Chronic pain is common as this condition worsens.

Bunions are primarily caused by improper biomechanics. Pronation is the main culprit. It causes excessive mobility of the first ray (*medial cuneiform, first metatarsal, first proximal,* and *distal phalanx*). With extra

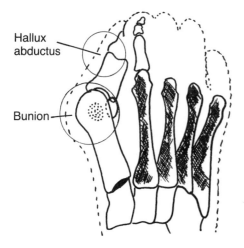

Hallux
abductus

Bunion

Bunion with hallux abductus

movement along the first *metatarsal* head, rubbing occurs against the shoe. A muscular imbalance will then pull the toe laterally.

It is important to start conservative treatment as early as possible. This could sidestep the need for surgical correction. Make sure shoegear and stockings fit correctly; these external forces can increase the formation of the bunion.

When abnormal pronation is present, the use of biomechanical orthotic devices are extremely important. They can correct the abnormal muscular imbalances and stabilize the positions of the bones and joints. Chronic, painful bunions eventually will require surgical correction. If the joint is involved, that probably will end a dancing career. Conservative treatment at an early stage is the best alternative.

BURSITIS

Bursitis is the inflammation of a *bursa,* a small sac in the fibrous tissue that contains fluid. Bursae are located at areas where there is much pressure or friction. They protect the underlying tissue and allow free movement without straining or stretching the tissue. They act as shock absorbers to many of the joints of the foot protecting the bones. They develop under corns, bunions, and other areas where bone pressure is excessive.

A trauma or overuse of the affected part will cause the sac to become enlarged and inflamed. Additional fluid fills the sac as bursitis develops. Most commonly affected areas are behind and below the heel, under the first *metatarsal* head, in the bunion area, and in the toes.

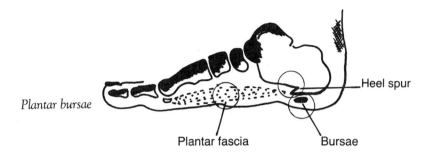

Plantar bursae — Heel spur

Plantar fascia   Bursae

Treatment includes resting the affected area. Removing weight bearing is also helpful. Proper strapping and padding can accomplish this goal (see Chapter 5). Injection and physical therapy can help reduce the swelling and break down the bursal sac. They also increase circulation to the area to speed healing.

A biomechanical exam and gait analysis is usually necessary. When the cause of the bursitis is related to faulty biomechanics, orthotics can control this abnormality. By stopping the abnormal forces, recurrence of the bursitis should be minimized.

Surgery sometimes is necessary when the underlying cause is the anatomy of the bone structure. Usually, reshaping of the underlying bone can prevent the bursitis from occurring.

CALLUS AND CORNS

Callus and *corns* are the buildup of hard skin with an accumulation of keratin in the *epidermis*. They are the direct result of pressure, stress, or friction, usually from abnormal foot mechanics. Both conditions are composed of the same material. Callus form in a flat, straight pattern similar to the normal skin lines. Corns are conical or circular in formation. They can be pushed deeper into the skin and cause more pain. A soft corn is located in the interspace between the toes.

Some dancers will form a normal amount of superficial callus. This is a direct response to the increased friction and pressure of dancing on the foot. This superficial callus does not require treatment and should not be removed.

A *shearing callus* and any type of corn can be very painful. They are abnormal formations that require treatment and should be removed for the dancers comfort. The pain can cause limping and compensation that could cause a secondary problem to develop.

When hard skin on the foot is causing pain, see a podiatrist. They can use surgical instruments to remove the lesions. Padding to disperse weight from the area can be helpful (see Chapter 5). Usually, the condition will recur. Routine treatment is recommended. If the cause of your problem is an underlying bony pathology, an ambulatory surgical correction might eventually be needed. The need for surgery is dependent on the frequency and severity of the problem.

It is never a good idea to use a razor blade or scissor to cut the hard skin yourself. A mistake can cause a very painful infection and loss of dance time. Self-treatment includes soaks, the use of a pumice stone or callus file and over-the-counter padding material. They are safe to use if you follow the instructions.

Some people respond very well to the use of orthotics (see Chapter 5). They redistribute abnormal weight distribution and can reduce abnormal friction. Again, it is important to have proper fitting hosiery and shoegear. Prevention of the deforming forces can solve the problem.

CAPSULITIS

A *capsule* is a ligamentous bag that surrounds a joint. It is attached by its edge to the bones on either side. With excessive force, landings, or a trauma, the capsule can become inflamed, a condition called *capsulitis*. It fills with fluid and becomes very painful on palpation or as the joint is put through a range of motion.

The harder the dancing surface, the greater the chance that capsulitis will affect an involved joint. The first *metatarsal-phalangeal* joint is the most common site for capsulitis in the foot. This is where most weight-bearing occurs at toeoff (just before the toe leaves the ground in the gait pattern). Properly protecting the joints of the foot and dancing on a surface with more give are preventative measures.

Capsulitis requires medical intervention. The area should be padded and a strapping applied for protection (see Chapter 5). It is important to limit joint motion to allow for healing. Physical therapy is effective at reducing the inflammation. Injection therapy and anti-inflammatory medication are sometimes necessary. For chronic sufferers of capsulitis, a biomechanical exam and gait analysis are important. If an underlying structural problem exists, it should be treated to prevent the excessive joint force. Normally, capsulitis responds to treatment in about two weeks. Dancing should be limited during the healing time.

CONTUSIONS

Contusions are soft-tissue bruises. The bruise does not affect the underlying bone or create a break in the skin. Capillaries (small blood vessels) rupture after a compression or shock to the foot. Dancers most frequently bruise the ball of the foot or the ends of the toes from landing. When a person jumps, the force hitting the foot increases four times; therefore, 150-pound person lands with a force of 600 pounds. It is easily understandable why contusions can occur.

Immediate treatment for a contusion is "ICE" therapy (ice, compression, elevation) for the first 24 to 28 hours. Then, heat should be used to improve healing. Dispersion padding can protect the immediate area (see Chapter 5). A hematoma (blood clot) might form, which will increase the pain greatly. The use of heat should help break up the clot (see *Hematomas*). Loss of dance time is only a few days, but protecting the area will prevent recurrence.

DISLOCATIONS

A *dislocation* occurs when bones separate at a joint but do not fracture. Any joint in the foot can dislocate. The most common for a dancer is a dislocation of one of the toe joints. Any dislocation will cause a great amount of pain and swelling.

ICE therapy should be started quickly: ice applied to the area, compression of the involved joint, and elevation. Immediate medical attention is needed to put the bones back into position. This can be done manually, sometimes with anesthesia, and sometimes surgically.

Once the bones are back into their normal alignment, there still will be swelling and pain in the joint. The trauma to the joint will cause a capsulitis condition (see *Capsulitis*). Injection with anti-inflammatories and anesthetics, physical therapy, and strappings for immobilization are very helpful. The severity and layoff from dancing depends on the specific injury and bones involved.

EXOSTOSIS

An *exostosis* is an overgrowth of bone in an area due to continued pressure. A spurring of bone develops as a response to the friction. The long growth causes pain when compressed against another bone or a shoe. The

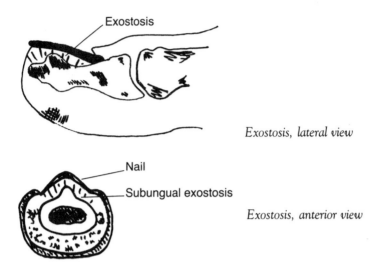

Exostosis

Exostosis, lateral view

Nail

Subungual exostosis

Exostosis, anterior view

continued pressure can cause bursitis to form in the soft tissue, the exostosis, and the skin. When the bony growth is under a toenail it is called a *subungual exostosis.* Arthritis and other conditions can cause spurs to occur anywhere in the foot. The most common place for a dancer to develop an exostosis is in the toes. Corns in the toes are often caused by an exostosis.

Conservative treatment includes padding around the bony growth to reduce friction (see Chapter 5). Injection therapy and physical therapy can decrease the pain from the bursitis. Avoiding pressure across the exostosis should reduce symptoms. Wearing proper fitting shoegear is essential (see Chapter 2).

Surgical correction is sometimes necessary. Removing the bony growth will return the natural shape of the bone. This is the best way to control an exostosis in the long term. In most cases, the procedure can be done in the office. It is an ambulatory surgery; and only a few weeks of dance time is lost. It is recommended for people who have pain and the condition is chronic. It is an elective procedure that can be performed to fit in with the dancer's schedule.

FISSURES

Fissures are cracks that occur in the skin. They are especially prevelant in the heel area. Usually, they are caused by excessive dryness.

Dancers face the problem of developing cracks at the heads of the *metatarsals,* frequently associated with barefoot dancing. The ball of the

*P*atrick was performing with a modern dance company. For several years, he was being treated conservatively for a *heloma molle*, a soft corn. His lesions developed between the second and third toes. Treatment included debridement, or removal with a scapel, of the hard skin and the use of separators or lambswool to cushion the area. His visits for treatment were becoming more frequent, however, and the pain increasing.

X-rays revealed the cause of the problem. He had developed exostoses of bone on the second and third *proximal phalanx*. The two bumps of bone would pinch the soft tissue between them. The body's response was to try to protect and cushion the area. Hard skin was deposited and a bursal sac with fluid created. As the corn grew larger, more fluid would accumulate in the bursa from the increased pressure. The resulting bursitis was painful, but temporarily relieved when the corn was removed.

Patrick decided he wanted to correct this condition. The pain had gotten too great, and finding proper treatment while on the road was inconvenient. His condition was interfering with his ability to dance. We scheduled surgery when the company had a one-month break in their schedule. In my office, I removed both exostoses through small incisions. The bones were remodeled with a surgical drill in the same manner a dentist remodels a tooth.

After one week, I took the stitches out. For the first two weeks, Patrick was not allowed to dance. He still exercised and did his stretching. By the third week, he returned to floor exercises. By the fourth week, he returned to light dancing without jumps and any other traumatic movements. After four weeks, he was discharged and back to full dance. He would still experience occasional swelling and tenderness but was able to return to the company. Three weeks later, he called from Salt Lake City to let me know how great he felt.

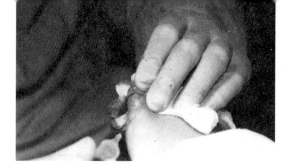

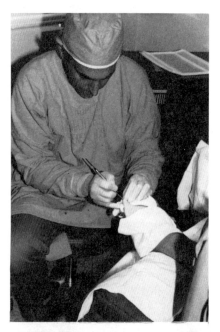

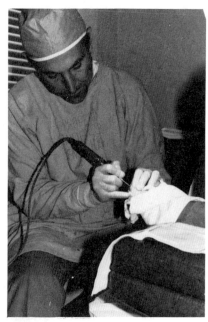

Dr. Spilken surgically removes an exostosis (overgrowth) of bone in the dancer's fifth toe. This type of ambulatory surgery allows the patient to return to dance very quickly. This dancer was back in class in two weeks. Photo by Eric Shonz.

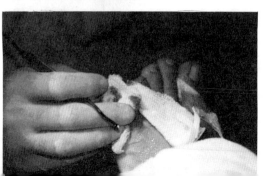

foot acts as a pivot and can be subjected to great forces and friction with the dance floor. When the skin cracks, it can cause a great deal of pain and loss of dance time.

The best prevention for fissures is to keep the feet moist, except before dancing. This can be accomplished with frequent use of moisturizing cream and skin lubricants. Once a crack develops, keep it clean and use antiseptics. An antibiotic ointment should be applied with a bandage covering the area. Dance can be resumed when the area is free from pain. If you chronically suffer from this problem, use of moleskin or tape over the affected area will reduce the friction and decrease the chance of recurrence. Use zinc oxide ointment to protect the skin before putting a protective covering over the area.

FOREIGN BODIES

A *foreign body* is any object penetrating the skin that does not belong there. This happens most frequently for barefoot dancers. A foreign body could be a splinter of wood or other material, piece of glass, a needle or pin, sand, debris of all sorts, slivers of numberous objects, even human hair. Once the foreign body enters, the body will try to encapsulate the intruder. A chronic foreign body could cause a cyst to form around it (*epidermal inclusion cyst*).

The immediate problem is pain and the chance of infection. The pain can be very intense when weight-bearing or pressure is exerted in the area. The bacteria present in the object will try to grow under the skin. Self-treatment would include trying to remove the object with a sterile instrument after a good antiseptic cleaning. Proper antibiotics and a dry sterile dressing is very important. Do not hesitate to receive proper medical attention when necessary. The relief is immediate and dancing may resume at once.

FRACTURE

A *fracture* is a bone break. A bone can chip, splinter, compress, break into many pieces, or compound (stick out of the skin). The type of fracture will depend upon the activity at the time of the injury and the position of body weight. The extent of the injury and amount of down-time from dancing depends upon the type of fracture and which bone or bones are involved.

ICE therapy should be started immediately: ice the area of injury, use compression and around it, and keep it elevated. Seek medical attention just as quickly. Many dancers injure their feet and deny the

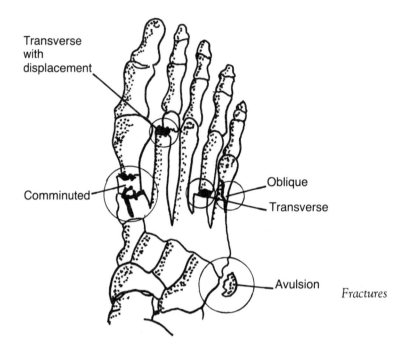

Transverse with displacement

Comminuted

Oblique

Transverse

Avulsion

Fractures

seriousness of the incidence. Any injury causing pain, swelling, tenderness, or an inability to bear weight should be seen by a specialist. The longer treatment is delayed, the longer healing will take.

X-rays must be taken to rule out a fracture with any bone injury. If the bone is displaced, it could require setting (reduction), possibly performed surgically. The bone must be immobilized for proper healing. Depending on the bone involved, healing can take four to six weeks. The immobilized bone should be allowed to rest without continuous force. Thus, dancing must be stopped for proper healing. The only exceptions to this rule are some of the bones in the toes or the sesamoids under the first *metatarsal*. A visit to an emergency room, when your doctor is not available, should be followed by a visit to your podiatrist. Follow-up care and evaluation after a bone injury is a necessity.

Physical therapy should be combined with after-care visits for prompt healing. Traumatic arthritis could develop after a fracture and limit joint movement and create pain. Follow all medical instructions carefully and a gradual return to dancing should occur.

GANGLIONS

A *ganglion* is an enlargement of a tendon sheath (covering of the tendon) or joint sac that fills with fluid. Trauma to the sheath or sac causes the ganglion to form. A ganglion is a type of *cyst*, a sac that forms under the skin that contains fluid or soft material. Irritation to an area can cause a cyst to form.

The ganglion is usually slow growing and is soft and freely moveable. Pain occurs when pressure is exerted over the mass. The most common spot for a ganglion to form is above the extensor tendons on the dorsum of the foot. Pressure from a shoe across this area should be avoided.

Treatment includes padding around the ganglion to avoid direct pressure. Injections with steroids can help break the walls of the ganglion and promote reabsorption of the fluid. Sometimes, aspiration with a needle to drain the cyst is needed. Tight compression bandaging is then applied.

When conservative therapy is unsuccessful and pain persists, surgery is recommended. Thus, the entire sac and its contents are removed.

HAMMER TOES

A *hammer toe* is a condition where the toe bends into a shape similar to the end of a hammer. The top or end of the toe can receive excessive pressure because of this abnormal shape. This pressure can cause the toe to become red, swollen, blister, or form hard skin or a corn.

Hammering of a toe usually is caused by a muscular imbalance due to bone structure and the positioning of the tendons. When these tendons pull, they create an uneven pull on the bone. With time, the

Hammer toe

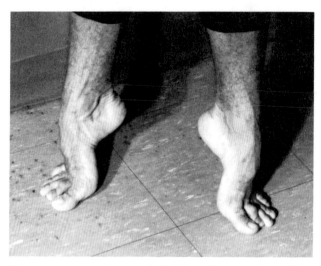

Hammer toe: second toe on the left foot shown in relevé. Note how the third, fourth, and fifth toes remain on the floor in an extended position.

bone position will actually change. This is a hereditary tendency that you cannot control.

The other leading cause of hammer toes is an outside force. A toe will bend if the shoe is too snug. Constant force against the toes will eventually cause a hammer toe. This you can control. Make sure your shoes do not jam against the foot. Read the section on correct fitting of shoegear.

Biomechanical orthotic devices will help the muscular imbalances and poor boney anatomy. Surgery should only be considered for the chronic, painful condition that might develop; Surgery for cosmetic purposes is not recommended.

HEEL SPURS

A *heel spur* is an overgrowth of bone in the heel. It usually occurs on the medial side of the *calcaneus* (heel bone) on the plantar aspect. It occurs on the tuberosity of the bone where the *plantar fascia*, or sole's connective tissue, originates.

The cause of a heel spur is usually an abnormal pull of the plantar fascia. As the fascial band pulls, fibers start to tear off the attachment in

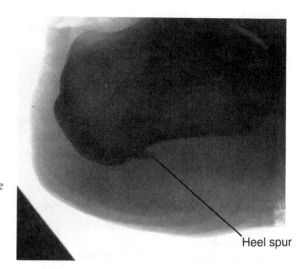

Polaroid X-ray showing the formation of a heel spur under the heel bone.

Heel spur

the *calcaneus*. The body fills these tears with new bone. It is also trying to shorten the stretch on the *plantar fascia* by shortening its distance.

The pain from a heel spur is from the formation of new bone. Usually a bursitis forms or a nerve entrapment occurs. A fully formed heel spur usually becomes asymptomatic. Unfortunately, it takes years to fully form and the pain can be severe during this period.

Heel spurs are usually associated with a complete syndrome that includes bursitis and plantar fasciitis. Initial treatment attempts to treat the acute pain with injection and physical therapy. Padding and strapping of the foot are very helpful (see Plantar Fasciitis). Anti-inflammatory medications are also very helpful.

Heel spurs usually result from faulty biomechanics. A complete biomechanical exam and gait analysis should be performed. Excessive pronation causing the abnormal pull of the plantar fascia should be treated with orthotics. Correctly aligning the feet will prevent the abnormal force and, within a few weeks, stop the pain. With proper conservative therapy, surgery will be almost completely unnecessary. Only 5 percent of the population does not respond and will require surgical removal of the bony spur and cutting of the fascia band.

Dancing might have to stop for a short time to allow the area to rest. With proper treatment, however, only a few days of dancing usually will be lost. Certain movements of the foot cause excessive pronation and should be avoided. *Pliés* top the list and lands from jumps involving the heels should be avoided.

HEMATOMAS

A *hematoma*, or blood clot, is an accumulation of blood in an area. A capillary will break, usually because of a trauma, repetitive force, or friction. The blood that spills stays in the area without any external bleeding. The primary area in the foot affected by hematomas are the toes and toenails.

Hematomas in the toes usually occur because of quick stops. The toe and toenail are jammed into the end of the shoe. Obviously, a dancer in an improperly fitting shoe is more susceptible to this condition. The nail can become disfigured from the pressure or the entire nail can be lost.

When the accumulation of blood is under the toenail, it is called a *subungual hematoma.* Subungual hematomas can be very painful. Pressure is exerted on the nail bed from the accumulation of blood. To stop the pain, the pressure must be released. A hole is made in the nail to allow the blood to escape. The pain usually will disappear immediately. Proper use of antibiotics and a dry sterile bandage should prevent infection. One can return to dance immediately after treatment.

Hematomas in other parts of the foot should be treated with heat. Apply heat to the area for 10 to 15 minutes every hour. Moist heat works better than dry heat. Protect the area to disperse weight off of the hematoma. Dancing can continue without any interuption unless pain persists.

Prevention is easier than treatment. Keep the nails cut short and even. Cut the nails straight across without cutting into the sides. Try to always wear proper fitting shoegear and socks. Keep shoes in good condition and replace when necessary.

INFECTIONS

Infections of the foot are caused by bacteria. The bacteria enter through a break in the skin. The area appears red, hot, and swollen, and pus may be present. One can even have an elevated body temperature as your white blood cells battle the bacteria. Infections around the nail beds and on the plantar aspect of the foot are especially painful. They can easily cause loss of dance time due to the pain.

Infections can be very dangerous. The bacteria can spread up the ankle into the leg and into the entire body. This condition is called an *ascending cellulitis*, leading to a septic condition. Infections caused by foreign bodies can be especially dangerous. Tetanus is a possibility that is life threatening. Because of the frequency of barefoot dancing, tetanus immunization is particularly important for a dancer.

Immediate attention is needed for any infection. Try soaks with Epsom salts and warm water. Topical antibiotics should be applied and the area covered with a dry sterile dressing. If the area does not respond quickly, seek medical attention.

A podiatrist will probably do a culture and sensitivity test. This will isolate the infective organism and determine the best antibiotic. An oral antibiotic will prevent the spread of infection. An incision and drainage should be performed to allow the area to heal. If the infection is caused by an offending nail particle or foreign body, it will be removed. Relief is almost immediate. Return to full dancing is usually within a day or two.

INGROWN NAILS

The corner of a nail can grow into the skin, causing an *ingrown nail*. Any pressure across an ingrown nail will elicit pain. If the nail punctures the skin, an infection will develop. This is called a *paronychia*.

Ingrown nails can be caused by improper shoegear or stockings. This causes pressure on the nail plate and changes the normal growth of the nail. Cutting the nails incorrectly is another leading cause of ingrown nails. Cutting into the corner of the nail may leave an edge that grows into the skin. When you cut your toenails, always cut them straight across.

Treatment begins with warm soaks with Epsom salts. A visit to a podiatrist is a must. Early treatment usually will mean no loss of dance time. The doctor will remove the offending nail particle and use appropriate antibiotics when necessary. The chronic sufferer can undergo a minor office procedure done to prevent the recurrence of this condition.

KNEE INJURIES

A dancer's foot book would not be complete unless it discussed knee problems. A dancer's knee is second only to the foot in vulnerability. Here, only knee injuries due to abnormal biomechanics of the foot will be covered.

In ballet position, 180-degree turnout at the hip is required. Dancers who cannot reach 180 degrees will force their knees and ankles out to try to create the appearance that the hip has rotated. The dancer will bend the knee to accomplish fifth position. This results in instability in the knee and strain on the ligaments. More important, there is a great chance for injury.

The *grand plié* puts extreme pressure on the knee. The dancer is bending the knee fully in the five positions of ballet. Pressure is exerted on the *tibial collateral ligament,* and ligament and cartilage damage can develop. Moderation is the key word; repetition could lead to serious knee injury. Avoid sitting in this position.

The most common knee injury for a dancer is due to an overuse syndrome. We call it "dancer's knee" or *chondromalacia patella.* It is most commonly caused by excessive and abnormal pronation of the foot. This excessive foot movement will cause a twisting in the knee from minor rotational changes. The mobile and flexible foot type will develop medial and anterior knee pain. The dancer with a more rigid and inflexible foot has limited motion and greater shock on impact and usually develops lateral knee pain. Because of their wider hips, women tend to have more problems with dancer's knee.

Treatment for this condition involves controlling the abnormal biomechanics. Wearing orthotics while dancing and in regular shoegear controls the excessive pronation and reduces the abnormal force on the knee. Early diagnosis and treatment will prevent more permanent damage.

LACERATIONS

Lacerations are cuts in the skin, a break in the epidermis. This is not a common dancer's injury. A minor laceration needs basic first aid and bandaging. If treated promptly, the chance of an infection developing is very small.

If the cut is deep enough, sutures will be needed. Loss of dance time could be a few days to a few weeks depending upon the location. When the cut is near a joint, splinting is usually needed to allow the area to heal properly. Infections should be treated seriously (see Infections).

MORTON'S FOOT

This is a biomechanical condition named after Dr. Dudley J. Morton. It has widely been considered a leading cause of pain and problems in the world of sports medicine. A Morton's foot is demonstrated by a short first *metatarsal.*

Sally was an aerobics dance instructor. Her problem was in her right knee. Pain occurred as each class neared the end or on days when she tried to teach two classes. She was experiencing pain in the middle and toward the bottom of her knee. The pain would get so bad that she had to stop teaching. In spite of any treatment she rendered, as her workout increased, the pain would return.

She was referred to me by an orthopedist. His examination did not reveal any pathology in her knee. He believed her problem was related to her foot structure—a correct diagnosis. She had *chondromalacia patella* (dancer's knee, runner's knee.) Chondromalacia is a wearing away of the cartilage in the knee. It was caused by Sally's excessive pronation.

A biomechanical exam and gait analysis revealed the problem. As her right heel hit the ground it was in an inverted postion. For the heel to flatten, the entire foot had to pronate over and evert. Her entire leg, along with her knee was also rolling inward. When standing, her right knee was facing in the direction of her left foot. In neutral, the right knee should point directly over the right foot. The excessive motion caused the *patella*, or anterior bone of the knee, to rub. After enough activity, the pain would start.

Her treatment was simple. I fabricated a sports orthotic to stop the excessive pronation. It controlled her rearfoot *varus* and prevented the extra movement in her knee. Within a month, her pain totally disappeared. Now, she uses her orthotics every time she does aerobic dancing and has not had a reoccurrence of symptoms.

The normal parabola of the *metatarsal* heads would have the first *metatarsal* as the longest and the length of the other *metatarsals* decreasing towards the outside of the foot.

With a shorter first *metatarsal*, excessive pronation will occur. The body's weight distribution falls toward the inside of the foot. The dancer's balance will not be along the normal lines of the body. More weight is thrown into the arch area.

Medically there is a hypermobility of the first ray, which means excessive movement along the inner part of the foot. This extra motion makes the dancer more prone to forming bunions. There is also an increase in the work of the second *metatarsal.* As the longest *metatarsal,* it receives an increase in the stress through weight-bearing and liftoff during gait. The second *metatarsal* head usually hypertrophies and the shaft of the bone thickens. A painful lesion can occur on the bottom of the foot below the second *metatarsal* head. In addition, there can be a displacement of the two tiny sesamoid bones located under the first *metatarsal.*

A Morton's foot is an anatomical condition. Some dancers with this foot type can have a normal dance career. If symptoms develop, a restriction of certain dance movements might be necessary. Performing *relevés* correctly can become very difficult; distribution of weight on the ball of the foot becomes necessary.

Initial treatment usually involves the use of paddings and strappings to give additional support to the first *metatarsal* and take pressure off the second *metatarsal.* A review of your dance technique with a dance teacher is extremely important. Long-term use of orthotics for stability and for a decrease in abnormal motion and force is recommended.

NERVE ENTRAPMENTS AND COMPRESSION

Nerve entrapments can occur in the soft tissue of the foot. Nerve compression is also associated with this condition. These can occur from repeated severe pressure across the nerve. A direct trauma can also damage the nerve against the bone. Sometimes these nerve problems are secondary to other conditions (heel spurs, exostosis, or fractures). Entrapments imply that the nerve is not moving freely and is trapped in an area. Compression means that something is pressing on the nerve.

Nerve entrapments and compression occur mostly in dancers where there is constant pressure in an area. Shoegear consistently impinging on an area for an extended period can lead to this problem. Symptoms can include pain, numbness, a tingling sensation, and even muscle weakness.

Proper fitting shoegear is essential. Proper diagnosis is extremely important. When the nerve entrapment or compression is caused by another condition, prompt treatment should alleviate the nerve problem.

It is vital to establish the primary cause to correctly treat these symptoms.

Sponge rubber can be used to alleviate direct pressure from the affected area. Conservative therapy includes injections and physical therapy in an attempt to break up scar tissue or other inflammation that might be causing the problems. When all else fails, surgical intervention is necessary to free the nerve.

NEURITIS, NEURALGIA

Neuritis is an inflammation of a nerve. It is usually the nerve's covering (sheath) that is affected. Neuritis usually develops as a consequence of long-acting pressure and irritation of the nerve. Pain from neuritis is usually continuous.

Neuralgia is nerve pain without any change in the structure of the nerve. Neuralgia can be caused by direct trauma, foreign bodies, scars, exposure to cold and damp, diseased bone, or an inflammation of the nerve (neuritis). Because there are so many causes of neuralgia, it is important to find the primary condition causing the pain.

Neuritis and neuralgia require professional treatment. A dancer with nerve-like symptoms such as electric shock, loss of sensation, tingling, shooting pain, paralysis, and so on should immediately contact a physician. Conservative treatment with injections and physical therapy are helpful. The primary objective is to locate the cause of the nerve problem. (See Neuroma).

NEUROMA

A *neuroma* is a benign tumor. It is an overgrowth of nervous tissue usually caused by excessive pressure and irritation. The repetitive force to the covering of the nerve causes a mass of new nerve growth to form.

The most common area to form neuromas in the foot are between the toes, the areas called *interspaces*. There are four interspaces on each foot. Pressure between the heads of the adjacent *metatarsals* cause the neuroma to form. Usually, a dancer will form a neuroma between the third and fourth *metatarsal* in the third interspace.

Pain can be severe as the neuroma gets larger. It can be described as electrical shocks with shooting-type pain. Tingling and occasional loss of sensation can sometimes occur. Symptoms worsen when wearing shoes or with any confinement of the foot.

Neuromas diagnosed early usually respond well to conservative

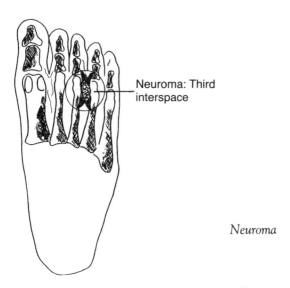

Neuroma: Third
interspace

Neuroma

therapy. Wider shoes to take pressure off the *metatarsals* help. A felt plug can be put under the head of an adjacent *metatarsal* to take pressure off the nerve. Injection therapy and physical therapy are also effective. Long-term use of orthotics to control any abnormal biomechanics is generally the best treatment plan. Surgery can be performed if all else fails. Because nerve tissue is removed in surgery, permanent loss of sensation in the interspace and into the toes is possible. Prompt conservative treatment is a much better alternative with virtually no loss of dance time (See Neuritis, Neuralgia).

PERIOSTITIS

Periostitis is a bone bruise. It occurs from a direct trauma to the bone. Bone is covered with a material called *periostium*. After a trauma to the bone, blood can fill into the space between the bone and its covering. The periostium is actually lifted off the bone.

This is a painful condition that should be differentiated from a fracture. X-rays should show the condition of the bone and the elevation of the periostium. The pain comes from the swelling to the surrounding soft tissue. Bone itself has no nerve endings and cannot feel pain.

The pain can limit dancing activities for up to two weeks. If the bone is actually fractured, there could be anywhere from four to six weeks of inactivity. The most common areas for a dancer to have a bone bruise is the heel and the *metatarsal* heads.

Immediate treatment can decrease the time needed for healing. The ICE regimen (ice, compression, elevation) should be started as quickly as possible. This might limit the amount of inflammation that causes the pain. Medical attention and X-rays are needed. Padding around the area can reduce the discomfort. Physical therapy, compression, medication, limitation of activities, and sometimes injection therapy are used in treatment. Periostitis untreated can cause pain for several months as compared to healing in about two weeks.

PLANTAR FASCIITIS

The *plantar fascia* is a long ligament on the bottom of the foot that attaches from the heel to the *metatarsal* heads. It helps create the arch of the foot and acts as a support for the anatomical structures of the foot.

Plantar fasciitis is an inflammation of this fascia band. It usually is caused by an abnormal pull of the ligament. The result is arch pain and sometimes pain in the area of the heel where the ligament attaches.

Two major causes for plantar fasciitis are biomechanical conditions and trauma. Any traumatic event to the arch area of the foot can cause inflammation of the fascia band. The most common cause of this type of trauma for a dancer involves jumps. Propelling off the ball of the foot and landings can cause abnormal strain. An incorrect landing can cause excessive trauma.

A biomechanical condition such as excessive pronation causes a stretch and lengthening of the foot. With repetitive occurrences of this pronatory force, the plantar ligament is stretched. As the abnormal force continues, the fascia band is strained and inflammation occurs. Dancers involved with any running routines are more likely to experience this problem. In addition, *pliés* involve excessive stretch on the arch. Incorrectly performing a *plié* can cause plantar fasciitis.

The immediate treatment is ice therapy (10 to 15 minutes of ice every hour) and limited activity during the first 24 to 28 hours. Rest is important during this time to limit the amount of swelling and prevent a more chronic situation. A podiatrist can apply various types of paddings and strappings to the foot for additional support. Probably, the best results are received by a long arch pad with a low-dye or rest strap. For the next few weeks, ice should be used immediately before and after dancing for 10 to 15 minutes. Anti-inflammatory medication and physical therapy sometimes are needed.

If a dancer is chronically developing a plantar fasciitis, a biomechanical exam and gait analysis is recommended. When a biomechanical fault is present, appropriate treatment is necessary. Usually, orthotics can stop the excessive motion and prevent the reoccurance of pain. If the chronic plantar fasciitis is traumatic in nature, there is a good chance that the problem lies in your dance technique. A dance teacher should be able to find the mistake that is causing the abnormal force.

SESAMOIDITIS

Two small bones called *sesamoids* are located under the head of the first *metatarsal*. They act as a fulcrum for the *flexor hallucis longus* tendon that passes through them to make it easier for the big toe to bend. Trauma to the ball of the foot can cause the sesamoids to inflame causing sesamoiditis. Fracture of a sesamoid can also cause this condition.

Landings from a jump are the primary cause of sesamoiditis. The dancer with a high arch (*cavus* foot type) is more susceptible. The sesamoids are more prominent in the high-arch foot. Performing incorrect turns or dancing on a surface that has no give are also contributing factors.

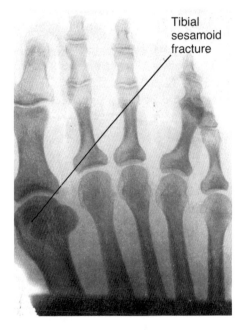

Tibial
sesamoid
fracture

Polaroid X-ray showing the tibial and fibular sesmoids. The tibial sesmoid shows a fracture.

*T*ony had been gradually experiencing arch pain over several months. The pain was at its worst during a *demi-plié*. Soon the pain was prevalent from walking and standing with dancing only intensifying the condition.

A biomechanical exam and gait analysis revealed excessive pronation with a rearfoot *varus*. His diagnosis was plantar fasciitis. With each step, the fascia band was being excessively pulled. Movements that flattened the foot (such as *demi-plié*) caused a greater force throughout the area. The plantar fascia was being overworked and becoming inflamed.

Acute treatment included physical therapy and strapping. That helped reduce his immediate discomfort. Still, I had to control his abnormal gait pattern to truly correct this condition. The solution was biomechanical orthotic devices. By fabricating orthotics, I was able to stop the abnormal strain and force in the arch area. The orthotics fit comfortably in his jazz shoes. He started using the orthotics and has not had a return of symptoms. Tony also claims that his legs and back do not feel as much force on them as before therefore do not fatigue as quickly.

Inflammation of a sesamoid will interfere with normal walking; dancing becomes almost impossible. Treatment by a podiatrist is essential for a quick return to performance. Immediate treatment is ice, compression, and elevation (ICE). After 48 hours, heat should be used. Protective dispersion padding should be used with a supportive strapping. Injection therapy and physical therapy are good treatments to speed healing time. Sometimes anti-inflammatory oral medication is necessary to reduce edema and pain. Treatment should take about two weeks.

People with a *cavus* foot type should take extra precautions to protect the sesamoid area. Dispersion pads can alleviate the direct force on the sesamoids. Orthotics can be devised to correct the abnormal foot position and alleviate the abnormal force.

SHINSPLINTS

Shinsplints are an overuse compartment syndrome. An overuse injury is exactly that: the muscles in an area are overused and fatigued. In shinsplints, the leg muscles are overused. The leg muscles are pulled away from their attachments into the tibia. Another theory is that the pain is in the muscle compartment itself from fatigue.

Shinsplints can affect different areas of the leg. Anterior shinsplints create pain on the lateral side of the leg. The anterior muscles raise the foot into dorsiflexion. Excessive pulling of these muscles leads to pain. Medial shinsplints cause pain on the inside portion of the tibia.

Posterior shinsplints cause pain in the back of the leg. The muscles travel down the back of the leg into the inside of the arch. Pronation causes the arch to flatten, putting a strain and a pull on these muscles. The pull extends into the muscle in the back of the leg.

Pronation can also cause anterior shinsplints. The anterior muscles work unconsciously to stabilize the foot, trying to hold the foot in the correct anatomical position. This extra work causes fatigue of the muscle group. Instead of propelling off the toes, the pronated foot is raised by the leg muscles.

Shinsplints are also caused by an imbalance between the anterior and posterior leg muscles. Most dancers develop very powerful posterior muscles in the leg. The anterior muscles work much harder because of the strength of the calf muscles. These muscles work in tandem. When the posterior group tightens, the anterior group must stretch. An imbalance of strength or flexibility between these muscles will cause fatigue from overuse.

The dance surface can also become a factor. The harder the floor, the more force exerted into the leg. The anterior muscles can tighten up to "splint" the foot in anticipation of the trauma of running or jumping on hard surfaces. Try to dance on as soft a surface as possible.

Shinsplints for a dancer can also be directly related to the position of the heel. A very popular theory is that shinsplints result if the heel does not make contact with the ground when landing. A proper landing from a jump should distribute the weight from the toes to the forefoot, midfoot, and finally into the rearfoot. The heel should be on the ground supporting body weight. A lack of heel contact causes all the force to stay in the forefoot. The only means of stability at this point are the leg muscles. They tighten and overwork, causing fatigue.

There is also a theory about double-heel strike. The heel reaches the ground then lifts slightly for balance after the landing. This creates a double-heel strike. The leg muscles work even harder for stability when this happens.

Treatment and prevention start with analyzing why the shinsplints are occurring. If technique is involved (landings, as an example), better training will help. If anatomical structure is involved, biomechanical orthotic devices are very helpful. By eliminating the unnecessary forces and excessive movement in the foot, there will be less strain on the leg muscles.

For immediate pain, RICE therapy is needed: Rest, apply ice, compression, and elevation. Ice can be applied immediately before and right after dancing, and again before bedtime. Dance can be continued to tolerance. Once pain starts, dancing should be stopped. Chronic shinsplints can lead to stress fractures.

It is important to be fully flexible. Stretch the leg muscles effectively to reduce extra pressure on the muscles (see Chapter 4). Try not to overstrengthen either the anteroir or posterior leg muscles. Each individual needs specific stretching or strengthening exercises depending upon their own needs. Eighty percent of all dancers respond well to flexibility training. Gradually build strength, coordination, and endurance of the leg muscles in an even manner.

SKIN RASHES

Many skin rashes can affect a dancer's foot. The discussions here will concern two categories. One will be the inflammatory conditions of the skin termed *dermatitis*. The other group will include rashes caused by organisms like fungus or yeast.

Dermatitis is a superficial skin inflammation. It is characterized by redness, blisters, scaling, swelling, oozing, crusting, and itching. Another term for this condition is *eczema*.

Dermatitis can be caused by contact with an external irritant. Contact dermatitis can be from a chemical reaction to any stimuli. The most common is from the dye in either shoegear or stockings. Some dancer's can have an allergic reaction to rosin or talc. They can react to a medication, cream, moisturizer, or other product they apply to their feet.

Dermatitis can also be the result of an allergic disorder. Dancers with hay fever or asthma are more prone to this reaction. They tend to break out in the soles of their feet and palms of their hands. The lesions can be itchy and annoying. Psoriasis and other dermatologic conditions can also be present.

The treatment for dermatitis involves discovering the causative factor. The source of irritant must be removed. Topical anti-inflammatory medication is prescribed. Usually, the patient responds in a few days and symptoms subside. Dancing can continue as tolerated. Bathing and use of soap on the area should be minimized. Sometimes an oral medication is needed to stop the itching.

The second category of skin rashes is caused by an organism, such as fungi and yeast. They are microscopic plantlike organisms that cause skin infections. The foot is a great host for these organisms; dark, warm, and moist.

The symptoms produced are similar to dermatitis: itching, inflammation, oozing, redness, blisters, and maceration. The maceration is usually between the toes and painful fissures can develop. The fungus can also lodge in the toenails. The nails get thick, discolor (yellow or brown), and debris forms under the nail.

If you develop a rash, it should be checked by a podiatrist. A culture can be taken to determine if an organism is present. Treatment includes use of antifungal topical agents. The feet should be kept dry, and walking barefoot will help keep the feet air dry.

The best treatment plan coincides with prevention. Good foot hygiene is essential. Daily bathing of the feet, keeping the feet dry, and wearing proper shoegear is important. Dry the feet thoroughly, especially between the toes. Daily use of foot powder is recommended. Changing shoes and socks regularly will decrease the chance for trouble to start. Use natural fibers (cotton, wool) because they are absorbent.

SPRAINS

A sprain is an injury to a ligament, nonelastic tissue that connects bone to bone, adding stability. The ligaments form the joints of the body. Any excessive pull or pressure on a joint area could lead to a sprain.

Sprains are classified into three grades. Grade one is a primary sprain in which there is no actual tear in the ligament. Mild to minimal tenderness with some swelling will occur. There is no instability of the affected joint. A secondary sprain has a partial or incomplete tear of the ligament. There is moderate instability of the joint. The pain is moderate with edema (black and blue), and difficulty bearing weight. Grade three involves a complete tear of the ligament. There is instability of the involved joint and the pain can be severe. Hemorrhage into the area is present and weight-bearing is virtually impossible.

Most sprains occur at the ankle. The majority of sprains at the ankle are inversion sprains (the foot rolls in). They are more common for the *cavus* foot type and the normal foot type. Eversion (foot rolls out) sprains are more common for the pronated foot.

Sprains at the ankle can be caused by many predisposing factors. Obviously, accidents occur. But as already indicated, certain foot types are more prone to ankle sprains. The dance surface is very important. An inclined or graded stage puts excessive pressure on the ankle. Certain dance movements will also put uneven pressure on certain areas. Constant changes in direction or non-natural movement will increase the chance for sprains to occur. Poor fitting or improper shoegear is also a prime factor.

Dancers are also affected by their own body structure. Forces can be exerted repetitively into an area because of the bony alignment. A muscular imbalance also can contribute to additional ligament stress. Ligamentous laxity with extensive ranges of motion add to instability.

A sprain can occur to any ligament. Treatment will depend upon the extent of damage. Immediate therapy follows the RICE guidelines: rest, ice the area, compression, and elevation. Professional treatment should be sought, X-rays are usually needed to rule out any fractures or dislocations. Immobilization and rest are essential ingredients for proper healing.

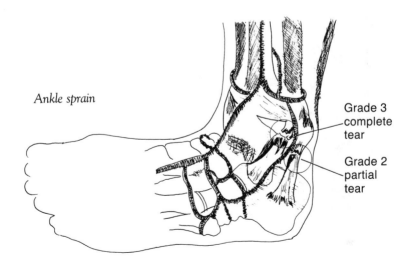

Ankle sprain

Grade 3 complete tear

Grade 2 partial tear

Grade one sprains require strapping and an elastic bandage or ankle brace. Healing occurs in under one week and a return to dance with full activities. Grade two sprains require a soft cast for immobilization from three to four weeks. Dancing should be avoided for at least two weeks and then only with permission from the doctor. Physical therapy is very helpful for both primary and secondary sprains. Grade three sprains require plaster casting and complete immobilization. Healing can take as long as eight weeks. Surgical repair is also a possible alternative. Unfortunately, surgery is difficult and results are not always satisfactory.

Prevention of the injury is more desirable than treatment. If anatomical structural deficiencies are present, biomechanical orthotic devices can be very helpful. They can stop some of the abnormal forces affecting the ligaments. Taping susceptible areas and devices like ankle braces will add external support.

STRESS FRACTURES

A stress fracture occurs from fatigue of the bone. Constant repetition of force on the bone will cause it to break. It starts as a microscopic fracturing with only a mild crack. As the force continues, the crack deepens and the fracture becomes more extensive. Overuse of one area can lead to the necessary force to cause a stress fracture. It is also called a "march" fracture from the repetitive force of marching.

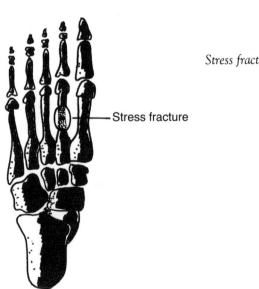

Stress fracture

Stress fracture

Stress
fracture

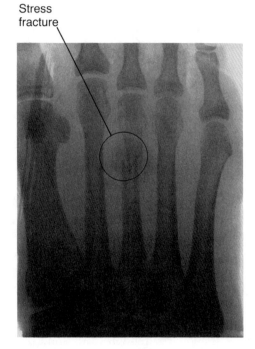

*Polaroid X-ray of a stress fracture of
the third metatarsal several weeks after
the dancer's symptoms started.*

Dancers most frequently develop a stress fracture of the second *metatarsal*. It can occur at any *metatarsal* or other bone of the foot or leg. Swelling and tenderness on palpation, and extreme pain are to be expected. Medical attention is needed.

Stress fractures usually do not show on an X-ray for two to three weeks. Even if the initial X-rays are negative, there is still the possibility of a stress fracture. Make sure you are seen by a podiatrist with a sportsmedicine background who can properly diagnose your condition. Stress fractures can be confused with capsulitis, bursitis, or tendonitis. Accurate diagnosis is essential because the treatment plan is different.

Treatment involves immobilization usually in a soft cast. Rest is very important and dancing should not be allowed. Weight-bearing in general should be limited. Nonweight-bearing exercise and stretching can be used during the layoff. The layoff usually lasts about four weeks. Injection therapy should not be used, but certain types of phyical therapy are helpful.

Once healed, a gradual return to full dancing is recommended. The causative factor must be identified and avoided or the condition can reoccur. A good biomechanical exam and gait analysis might be necessary. If a structural or anatomical position is causing excessive force, orthotics should be made to avoid continued pressure.

TENDONITIS

Tendonitis is an inflammation of the tendon. The foot has 19 tendons and their muscular attachments in each foot. A tendon attaches muscle to bone. When the muscle contracts, it causes a pull on the tendon that will move the bone.

A direct trauma to the tendon can cause it to inflame. Overuse of the tendon also causes tendonitis. This can occur from a change in workout techniques, learning a new dance step with repetitive movements, or a biomechanical imbalance causing the tendon to work harder than normal. An accidental movement or slip can also cause an unnatural force on the tendon.

Prevention is the key for any dancer. Correct stretching and flexibility can minimize the chances of inflamming a tendon (see Chapter 4). Proper warmup before and cool-down after dancing is vital.

Tendonitis results in pain when the tendon moves. Therefore, the primary objective of treatment is to stop the tendon from moving. This will allow the tendon to rest and facilitate healing. Proper strapping or casting is necessary for immobilization. Sometimes a pad can reduce the work of a tendon. A good example is the Achilles tendon. A heel lift pad will take some of the pressure off this very important tendon (see Chapter 5).

Immobilization might be necessary for as long as four weeks. Ice is used during the first 24 to 28 hours after the onset of pain. Heat is recommended after 48 hours have passed. Injection therapy and physical therapy are helpful. Anti-inflammatory medications sometimes are also necessary. The best treatment is still immobilization and rest. Without proper conservative therapy, surgery might be required to repair the tendon or remove scar tissue.

TINEA PEDIS

Tinea pedis is the Latin name for athlete's foot, a fungus infection that can affect the skin or nails of the foot. It can occur between the toes, on the bottom or top of the foot, or in the toenails. Dancers most commonly get this fungus in the arch area. Symptoms could include itching, scaling skin, burning, and redness. Blisters can form, and skin can become inflamed and

*E*liot, a 21-year-old male, had been dancing seriously for seven years. He was unhappy with the look of his jumps. Eliot decided to spend a full day just jumping. By early afternoon, he developed a throbbing-type pain near the ball of the right foot. Instead of stopping, he continued to work on his jumps. By late afternoon, the pain became so great he had to stop.

Eliot waited a few days for the pain to stop. Instead, it continued to get worse. He continued dancing in spite of the pain. A week later he finally came to my office. The diagnosis was a stress fracture at the neck of the second *metatarsal*.

The treatment plan was for four weeks of immobilization in a soft cast. After I applied the cast to his foot, Eliot asked an amazing question. "Can I dance today?"

It is always my highest priority to allow a dancer to continue dancing. Unfortunately for Eliot, it was not possible. Sometimes, complete rest is necessary to avoid more permanent damage. Eliot returned to full dance after the four weeks without any pain or problems.

---

oozing from the lesions may occur. Scratching the area could spread and worsen the condition. Another complication could be fissures (see Fissures). There is also a risk of developing a secondary bacterial infection.

Catching a fungus is similar to getting a virus; some people are more susceptible than others. Direct contact with the fungus is necessary but some people with higher resistance will not contract the condition. Fungus needs three things to survive: moisture, heat, and darkness. A foot in a shoe is a perfect environment for fungus to thrive.

Initial treatment can be with over-the-counter antifungal medications. Soaks can be very helpful to reduce the immediate itching. Powders should be used to keep the feet dry.

If the problem persists, professional help is needed. Strong prescription medications might be necessary. Prevention is important. Keep the feet as dry as possible. Use powder regularly to absorb perspiration and moisture. Use only natural fiber (cotton, wool) stockings

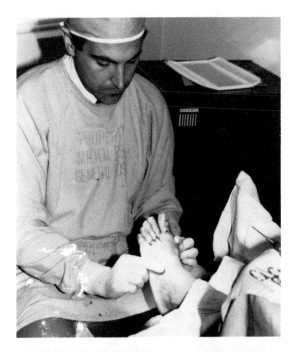

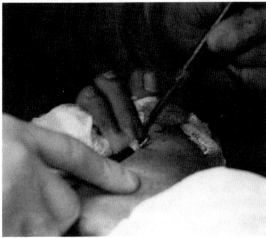

Dr. Spilken performs tendon surgery. A slip of the extensor digitorum longus has been exposed so an incision can be done on the tendon to lengthen its distance. Surgery should always be a last resort for a dancer after all conservative measures have been tried. Photo by Eric Shonz.

when possible. Because it is not absorbent, nylon and other synthetics retain moisture and heat against the skin.

VERRUCAE

Verrucaes are warts that can be found anywhere on the foot or body. When they are on the bottom of the foot, they are called *plantar's warts* (plantar means the bottom of the foot). *Verrucae vulgaris* occurs on the dorsum (top) of the foot. All warts are caused by the papova virus.

Plantar warts have a different appearance. Because you walk on them, they are flattened into the epidermis (skin layer). Warts are noninvasive. They grow only in the epidermis and do not invade into dermis or beyond. They can spread to other locations.

Warts are present mostly in adolescents but can affect any age group. Because they are caused by a virus, warts are contagious to susceptible people. A current theory is that a traumatized area can cause a weakening of resistance allowing the virus to take root.

Warts usually cause pain from squeezing, not on direct palpation. Warts are vascular (they have a lot of blood vessels). They can bleed very easily from rubbing or cutting. The pain occurs due to the pressure exerted by the wart's mass to the surrounding normal soft tissue.

Most over-the-counter treatments are not successful. Warts should be treated as soon as possible or they will increase in size and possibly spread to new locations. There are at least 20 forms of treatment, although none is 100 percent successful. Major surgical excision should be avoided. If a scar forms as a result of surgery, it could be a more painful condition than the wart.

Conservative therapy includes use of various acids. These treatments require weekly visits to the podiatrist and can continue for a long time. Your doctor should present you with several choices for treatment. Decide upon the best plan that least interferes with your dancing and lifestyle.

Alvin Ailey American Dance Center students at the June Gala performance. Photo by Marbeth.

APPENDIX I

DEFINITIONS FOR
THE FOOT
AND ITS MOTIONS

T he following list of definitions describes various parts of the foot and motions it goes through.

ABDUCTION. Motion occurring on the transverse plane during which the distal aspect of the foot (farthest part from the heart) or part of the foot moves away from the midline of the body.

ADDUCTION. Motion occurring on the transverse plane during which the distal aspect of the foot or part of the foot moves toward the midline of the body.

ANKLE JOINT. The joint between the *tibia, fibula,* and *talus* bones with the motions of dorsiflexion and plantarflexion, inversion, and eversion.

BOWLEG. See *Genu Varum.*

COMPENSATION. A change of structure, position, or function of one part of the body in an attempt by the body to adjust to or make up for an abnormal force from a deviation of structure, position, or function of another body part.

DISTAL. Farthest part away from the heart.

DORSUM. The top or anterior portion of the foot.

DORSIFLEXION. Motion occurring on the sagittal plane (up and down) during which the distal aspect of the foot or part of the foot moves toward the leg in an upward direction.

EQUINUS. A fixed structural limitation of dorsiflexion of the foot at the ankle joint. Any limitation preventing at least 10 degrees of foot dorsiflexion at the ankle when the subtalar joint is held in the neutral position.

EVERSION. Motion occuring on the frontal plane during which the plantar aspect of the foot or part of the foot is tilted so as to face further away from the midline of the body.

FLATFOOT. See *Pes Planus.*

FOREFOOT. Composed of the *metatarsal* and *phalange* bones; distal to the *metatarsal-cuneiform* and the *metatarsal-cuboid* joints.

FRONTAL PLANE. A flat vertical plane passing through the body from side to side, dividing it into a front half and a back half.

GENU VALGUM. An attitude of the knee joint in which there is eversion of the *tibia* on the *femur* (knock-knee).

GENU VARUM. An attitude of the knee joint in which there is inversion of the *tibia* on the *femur* (bowleg).

HYPERMOBILITY. Any motion in a joint during weight bearing when that joint should be stable under such load.

INVERSION. Motion occurring on the frontal plane during which the plantar aspect of the foot or part of the foot is tilted so as to face more toward the midline of the body.

KNOCK-KNEE. See *Genu Valgum.*

LATERAL. The side away from the midline of the body.

MEDIAL. The side toward the midline of the body.

MIDFOOT. Composed of the *medial cuneiform* (1), *intermediate cuneiform* (2), *lateral cuneiform* (3), *cuboid* and *navicular* bones; distal to the *midtarsal*

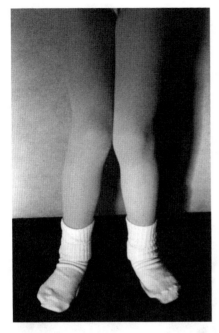 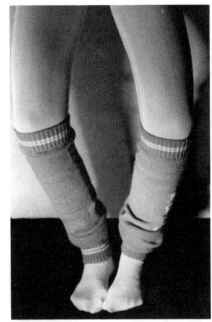

Genu valgum: knock-knee position of the legs   *Genu varum: bowlegged position of the legs*

joint and proximal to the *metatarsal-cuneiform* and *metatarsal-cuboid* joints.

MIDTARSAL JOINT. A series of joints between the rearfoot and the midfoot with the motion of pronation and supination.

NEUTRAL POSITION. That position of a joint when it is congruous in its range of motion and considered its best functioning position.

PES CAVUS. A high-arched foot.

PES PLANUS. A low-arched foot (flatfoot).

PLANTAR. The bottom or posterior portion of the foot.

PLANTARFLEXION. Motion occurring on the sagittal plane (up and down) during which the distal aspect of the foot or part of the foot moves away from the leg in a downward direction.

PRONATION. A triplane motion consisting of simultaneous movement of the foot of abduction, eversion, and dorsiflexion occurring in the subtalar and midtarsal joints.

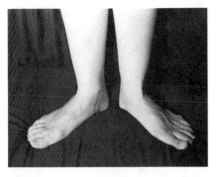

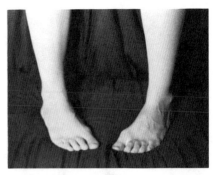

Abduction: toes pointing away from the body

Adduction: toes pointing toward the body

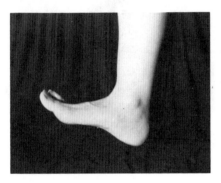

Dorsiflexion: toes pointing upward

Eversion: foot turning away from the body

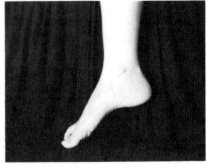

Inversion: foot turning toward the body

Plantar Flexion: toes pointing downward

PROXIMAL. Closest part to the heart.

REARFOOT. Consists of the *talus* and *calcaneus* bones; distal to the ankle joint and proximal to the *midtarsal* joint.

SAGITTAL PLANE. A flat vertical plane passing through the body from front to back dividing it into a right half and a left half.

SUBLUXATION. A gradual displacement in the integrity of a joint while in a state of hypermobility that results in eventual remodeling of the joint or dislocation.

SUBTALAR JOINT. The joint between the *talus* and *calcaneus* bones with the motion of pronation and supination.

SUPINATION. A triplane motion consisting of simultaneous movement of the foot or part of the foot in the direction of adduction, inversion, and plantarflexion occurring in the *subtalar* and *midtarsal* joints.

TIBIAL VARUS. A deviation of the lower third of the *tibia* in the direction of inversion.

TRANSVERSE PLANE. A flat horizontal plane that passes through the body from side to side and from front to back, dividing it into an upper half and a lower half.

VALGUS. A fixed structural position of the foot or a part of the foot that it would assume if it were everted (tilted away from the midline of the body).

VARUS. A fixed structural position of the foot or a part of the foot that it would assume if it were inverted (tilted toward the midline of the body).

APPENDIX II

FOOT ANATOMY

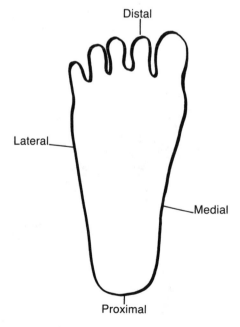

Plantar surface of the foot

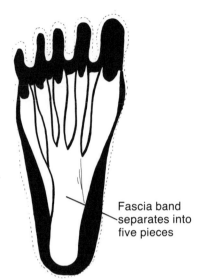

Fascia band
separates into
five pieces

Plantar fascia below skin on bottom of foot

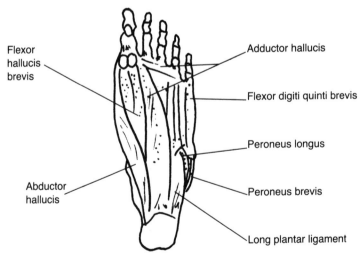

Flexor
hallucis
brevis

Adductor hallucis

Flexor digiti quinti brevis

Peroneus longus

Abductor
hallucis

Peroneus brevis

Long plantar ligament

Muscles and tendons of the foot, plantar view

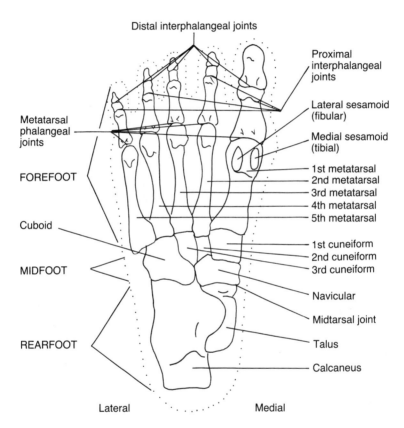

Bones of the foot, plantar view

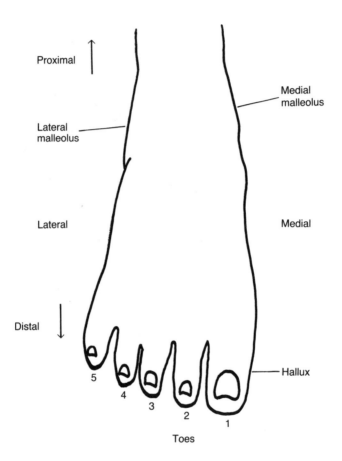

Dorsal surface of the foot

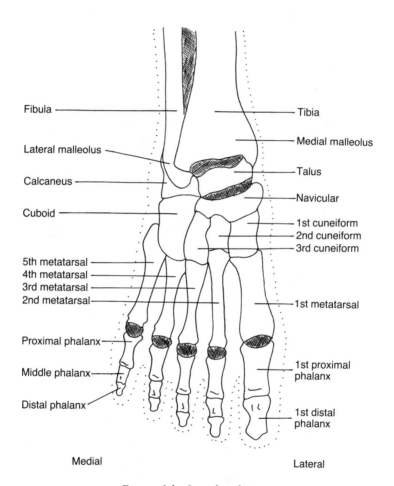

Fibula

Lateral malleolus

Calcaneus

Cuboid

5th metatarsal
4th metatarsal
3rd metatarsal
2nd metatarsal

Proximal phalanx

Middle phalanx

Distal phalanx

Tibia

Medial malleolus

Talus

Navicular

1st cuneiform
2nd cuneiform
3rd cuneiform

1st metatarsal

1st proximal
phalanx

1st distal
phalanx

Medial

Lateral

Bones of the foot, dorsal view

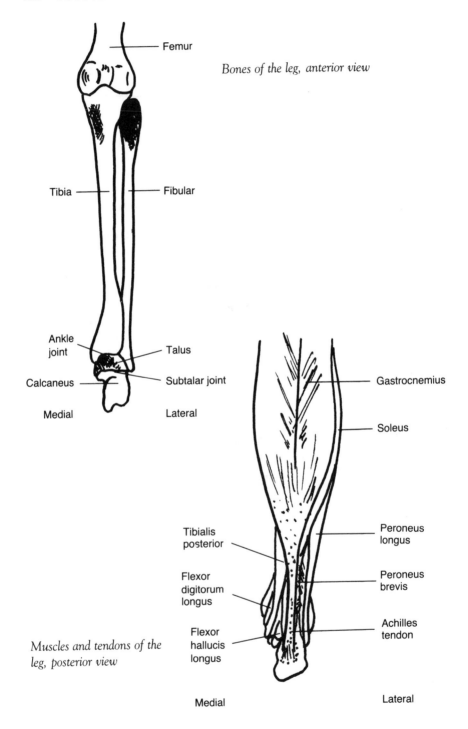

Femur

Bones of the leg, anterior view

Tibia

Fibular

Ankle joint

Talus

Calcaneus

Subtalar joint

Medial

Lateral

Gastrocnemius

Soleus

Tibialis posterior

Peroneus longus

Flexor digitorum longus

Peroneus brevis

Flexor hallucis longus

Achilles tendon

Muscles and tendons of the leg, posterior view

Medial

Lateral

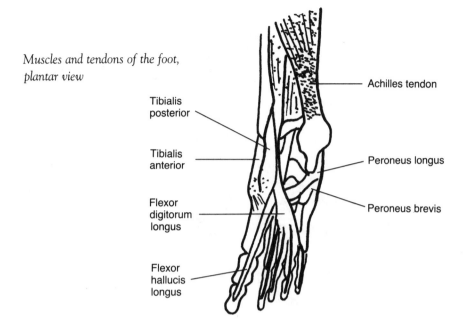

Muscles and tendons of the foot, plantar view

Tibialis posterior

Tibialis anterior

Flexor digitorum longus

Flexor hallucis longus

Achilles tendon

Peroneus longus

Peroneus brevis

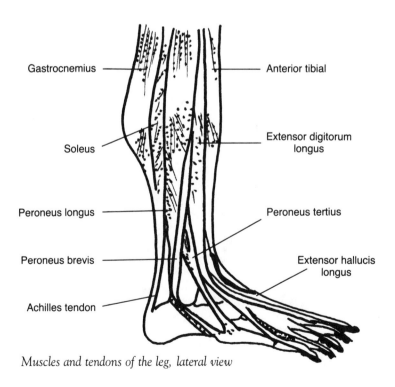

Gastrocnemius

Soleus

Peroneus longus

Peroneus brevis

Achilles tendon

Anterior tibial

Extensor digitorum longus

Peroneus tertius

Extensor hallucis longus

Muscles and tendons of the leg, lateral view

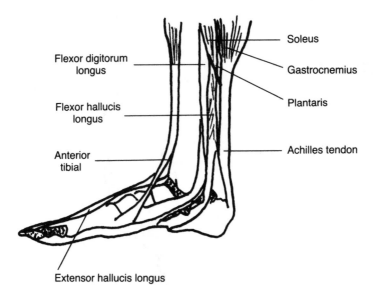

Muscles and tendons of the foot, medial view

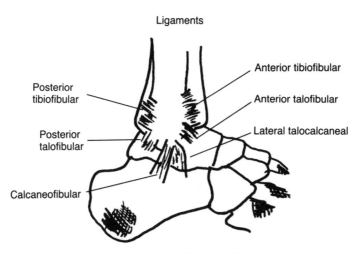

Ligaments of the ankle, lateral view

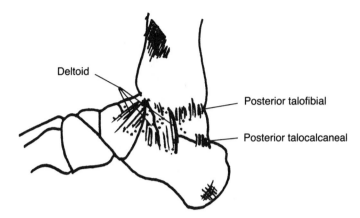

Ligaments of the ankle, medial view

NOTES

CHAPTER 1

1. Celia Sparger, *Anatomy and Ballet,* (New York: Theatre Arts Books, 1970), p. 38.

2. Ibid., p. 39.

CHAPTER 5

1. John E. McNerney and W. Bradley Johnston, "Generalized Ligamentous Laxity, Hallus Abducto Valgus and the First Metatarso-cuneiform Joint," *Journal of American Podiatry Association* 69, no. 1 (January 1979): 171.

2. James Kavanaugh, "First Ray," William B. School College of Podiatric Medicine, handout.

3. Ibid.

4. Ibid.

BIBLIOGRAPHY

Allen, Barbie. Barbie-Allen Dance/Exercise. Toronto: Personal Library, 1982.

Anderson, Robert. Stretching. Fullerton, Ca.: Robert A. Anderson and Jean E. Anderson, 1975.

Arnheim, Daniel D. Dance Injuries—Their Prevention and Care. Princeton, N.J.: Princeton Book Company, 1986.

Berkow, Robert, ed. The Merck Manual of Diagnosis and Therapy. Rahway, N.J.: Merck Sharp & Dohme Research Laboratories, 1977.

Cailliet, Rene. Foot and Ankle Pain. Philadelphia: F.A. Davis Co., 1975.

Fleming, Gladys Andrews. Children's Dance. Washington, D.C.: American Association for Health, Physical Education and Recreation, 1973.

Gamble, Felton O. and Irving Yale. Clinical Foot Roentgenology. Huntington, N.Y.: Krieger Publishing Co., 1975.

Gans, Aviva. "The Relationship of Heel Contact in Ascent and Descent from Jumps to the Incidence of Shinsplints in Ballet Dancers." Physical Therapy 65, no. 8 (August 1985): 1192–96.

Gelabert, Raoul. "Preventing Dancers' Injuries." *The Physician and Sports Medicine* 8, no. 4 (April 1980): 69–76.

―――. "The Myth of Dance-Induced Pain." *Dance* (May 1977): 96–97.

Giannestras, Nicholas J. Foot Disorders: Medical and Surgical Management. Philadelphia, Lea & Febiger, 1976.

Grant, J.C. Boileau. Grant's Atlas of Anatomy. 6th ed. Baltimore: Williams & Wilkins Co., 1972.

Hamilton, W.G. "Ballet and Your Body: An Orthopedist's View." *Dance* (August 1978): 81–83.

Hayes, Elizabeth R. An Introduction to the Teaching of Dance. New York: Krieger Publishing Co., 1980.

Hlavac, Harry F. The Foot Book: Advice for Athletes. Mountain View, Ca.: World Publications, 1977.

Hollander, Joseph Lee. The Arthritis Handbook. West Point, Pa.: Merck Sharp & Dohme, 1974.

Horosko, Marian and Judith R.F. Kupersmith. The Dancer's Survival Manual. New York: Harper & Row, 1987.

Humphrey, James H. Child Development and Learning Through Dance. New York: AMS Press, 1987.

Inman, Verne T. DuVries' Surgery of the Foot. St. Louis: C.V. Mosby Co., 1973.

Jessel, Camilla. Life at the Royal Ballet School. New York: Metheum Inc., 1979.

Kaplan, Charles, Peter D. Natale and Terry L. Spilken. Paddings and Strappings of the Foot. Mount Kisco, N.Y.: Futura Publishing Co., 1982.

Kelilian, H. Hallux Valgus: Allied Deformities of the Forefoot and Metatarsalgia. Philadelphia: W.B. Saunders Co., 1965

Kirstein, Lincoln. Ballet: Bias and Belief. Princeton, N.J.: Princeton Book Co., 1983.

Kranz, Hazel. "Dance Lessons for Little Children: Part Thirteen." *Dance* (January 1940): 17.

Lawson, Joan. Teaching Young Dancers. New York: Theatre Arts Books, 1975.

Leahey, Mimi. "Children on Their Toes." Chelsea Clinton News. 15 December 1983: 23–24.

LeBendig, Michael and Elliot Diamond. A Podiatric Resource Guide for Preventative and Rehabilitative Foot and Leg Care. Mount Kisco, N.Y.: Futura Publishing Co., 1976.

Mara, Thalia. First Steps in Ballet. 1955. Reprint Princeton, N.J.: Princeton Book Co., 1987.

———. The Language of Ballet: A Dictionary. Princeton, N.J.: Princeton Book Co., 1987.

———. Second Steps in Ballet. 1956. Reprint Princeton, N.J.: Princeton Book Co., 1987.

Mercado, O.A. An Atlas of Podiatric Anatomy. Third printing. Chicago, Ill.: National Academy of Hospital Podiatry, Illinois College, 1972.

Mirkin, Gabe and Marshall Hoffman. The Sports Medicine Book. Boston: Little, Brown & Co., 1978.

Missett, Judi Sheppard. Jazzercise Manual. Carlsbad, Ca.: Jazzercise Inc., 1986.

———. Jazzercise Student's Guide. Carlsbad, Ca.: Jazzercise Inc., 1986.

Parke, Janet L. To the Pointe. Memphis, Tenn.: Janet Parke, 1987.

Parks, Carolyn. "Toe Shoes When?" *Dance* (February 1953): Dance Magazine Reader Service Reprint.

Percival, Rachel. Discovering Dance. Philadelphia: Dufour Editions, 1966.

Rinaldi, Robert R. and Michael L. Sabia. Sports Medicine '78. Mount Kisco, N.Y.: Futura Publishing Co., 1978.

———. Sports Medicine '80. Part 2. Mount Kisco, N.Y.: Futura Publishing Co., 1980.

Roberts, Elizabeth. On Your Feet. Emmaus, Pa.: Rodale Press, 1975.

Rogers, Frederick Rand, ed. Dance: A Basic Educational Technique. New York: Dance Horizons, 1980.

Root, Leon and Thomas Kiernan. The Doctor's Guide to Tennis Elbow, Trick Knee, and Other Miseries of the Weekend Athlete. New York: David McKay Co., 1974.

Root, Merton L. et al. Normal and Abnormal Function of the Foot. Los Angeles: Clinical Biomechanics Corp., 1977.

Schneider, Harold J. et al. "Stress Injuries and Developmental Changes of Lower Extremities in Ballet Dancers." *Radiology* 113, no. 3 (December 1974): 627–32.

Sparger, Celia. Anatomy and Ballet. New York: Theatre Arts Books, 1970.

Stedman's Medical Dictionary. 22d ed. Baltimore: Williams & Wilkins Co., 1972.

Subotnick, Steven I. The Running Foot Doctor. Mountain View, Ca.: World Publications, 1977.

Switzer, Ellen. Dancers! Horizons in American Dance. New York: Anthenuem, 1982.

Thomas, William E. So You Want to be a Dancer. New York: Julian Messner, 1979.

Thomson, William. Black's Medical Dictionary. 31st ed. New York: Harper & Row, 1976.

Vagonova, A. Basic Principles of Classical Ballet. New York: Dover Publications, 1969.

Vincent, L.M. The Dancer's Book of Health. Princeton, N.J.: Princeton Book Co., 1988.

Warwick, Roger and Peter L. Williams. Gray's Anatomy. 35th British ed. Philadelphia: W.B. Saunders Co., 1973.

Wright, Stuart. Dancer's Guide to Injuries of the Lower Extremity: Diagnosis, Treatment and Care. Cranbury, N.J.: Cornwall Books, 1985.

Yale, Irving. Podiatric Medicine. Baltimore: Williams & Wilkins Co., 1974.

INDEX